THE SMART SCEPTIC'S GUIDE TO SOCIAL MEDIA IN ORGANISATIONS

Drive employee participation with real life insights and research

Yekemi Otaru

Foreword by Todd Wilms

"This book is a great synthesis of how social media can be applied in a B2B environment. I particularly like the point the author makes around making social media a shared ownership between all employees – and not just having it live an isolated life in some arbitrary marketing department. That simply undermines the authenticity and true premise for social media to be effective."

Klavs Valskov,
Branding Director at GE Oil & Gas

"*The Smart Sceptic's Guide to Social Media in Organisations* offers business leaders a structured approach to pursuing social media change management initiatives. Different to other books, case studies are intertwined with key insights and frameworks giving readers action orientated guidelines to put into practice in their organisations."

Dr. Jillian Ney, First doctor of social media in the UK,
Chief Intelligence Officer at Disruptive Insight

"*The Smart Sceptic's Guide to Social Media in Organisations* covers a topic that poses a constant question for business owners and managers: how to motivate their employees to use social media to promote the business – and protect their reputation.

Social media is so fast-moving, and such a world away from traditional PR, that it can be a very frightening place for a business which is new to this digital trend.

To some extent you are at the mercy of your employees – you have to put your trust in them and allow them to 'be social' whilst maintaining your brand. Better to have company guidelines in place and motivated employees who are trained to use social media effectively, than to stick your head in the sand and ignore it. There will be digital activity whether you like it or not – so far better to have some control.

The big question is how to create a flexible social profile and an ability to react quickly, within a corporate environment. How do you manage change? How do you introduce and encourage social media in a way that benefits the business?

These questions are all answered in this book. The book includes fascinating case studies showing practical examples and real life results.

I would recommend this book to anyone tasked with introducing social media to a business, anyone offering social media training in a corporate environment, as well as managers, sales and marketing teams."

Sara Greenfield, author of *LinkedIn Success Strategies,* *How To Tweet Your Book,* and social media expert

RƎTHINK PRESS

First published in Great Britain 2016
by Rethink Press (www.rethinkpress.com)

Cover image © Shutterstock.com/Paket

For my smart sceptics, Tonitse and Titi
– your questioning minds inspire me endlessly

CONTENTS

FOREWORD

What Do You Want To Build With Your Employees?

'There is this new thing called "Social Media",' said no company in the last three years. Hopefully, anyway. By now, most organizations have arrived at the conclusion that they need to do something about this thing called *social*, but many are still floundering. In fact, most companies follow the same basic processing on how to address social for their company:

Step 1: Finally agree that we need to do something about social media

Step 2: Build a team to do something about social media

Step 3: Team is less than successful because the goals are unclear

Step 4: Goals are established

Step 5: People are following your company. Check.

It is at this last step that the company has to make a decision – do we just want to check the box on social (make this the digital equivalent of billboards that scatter our highways) or do we truly want to engage with our community, our audiences.

I am excited about this book because so many want to do more with their company, their brand, their voice – but are unsure how to proceed. The next step is a Harrison Ford-ian leap into the abyss, hoping there is a path there to find the Holy Grail. There is tremendous pressure to communicate the value of your brand to your audience, and to hear back from them. The pressures are equal for both world-class brands and those that aspire to be. If you are already world-class, the stakes (and mistakes) are measured in billions. If you aspire to be world-class, the stakes can be more binary – success or failure before you really begin.

The brands that are doing this well take a page from the *Castellers'* playbook.

People can do some truly amazing things when we put our minds (and bodies) toward a common goal. *Castellers* are best described as human tower builders. At festivals around Catalonia, Spain, these *Castells* are created using only the strength and coordination of the team to get a tower crafted, up to nine-people high. Think about what it takes to get a single person to the top of a ladder of eight people, straight up, some 50 foot into the air. The spectacle of it is just as grand – a team all dressed alike, sporting their team colors, as the crowd cheers and supports their achievements. Amazing.

The really smart brands act like Castellers. They know the planning, support, and coordination it takes to do something amazing. They also understand that you can practice, practice, practice, but at some point, you are doing this live and in front of an audience.

Really smart brands realize that their employees are their best ambassadors, and that no social media team can accomplish by themselves what an entire company can do together.

But this might be the place where you have stalled. It is like seeing the tower built someplace else and you know it can be done, but getting your company to do it always ends up with everyone feeling kinda bruised.

You need the playbook from those that have 'been there, done that'. *The Smart Sceptic's Guide to Social Media in*

Organisations is exactly the playbook you have been looking for. Yekemi has spent years investigating, exploring, discussing what makes a brand fail, what makes them good, and what makes them great. These real-world examples from an amazing selection of brands help tell this story. From GE Oil & Gas to SAS to 'Marketing Consultant to the Stars' Krista Kotrla (she rocks!), this book will give you the insights you need and street cred you desire in your company to say, 'See, this really works!'

You can probably get a bunch of employees together in your backyard and build a human tower. It is theoretically possible that you can do that without any understanding of what it takes or how to do it. Chances are you will end up with your people on the ground looking like a game of Twister gone awry. Or, you can hear from people that have done it and done it well – and you can create something awe-inspiring and majestic.

Yekemi is on the path toward majestic.

Todd Wilms

VP Communications, Digital and Brand Marketing at Verisign, and Forbes Writer

PREFACE

This book is designed to help business-to-business corporations embark on social media programmes such as employee advocacy initiatives. But hang on: this book is not like any other book on social media that you've come across. It focuses on promoting and sustaining employee participation in your organisation. It's not about developing a social media strategy, nor does this book tell you how to use Twitter or Instagram or the likes. At the heart of social media is participation. That's what I'm passionate about – getting people to participate and collaborate within business-to-business (B2B) corporations. This book is unique because I use my original empirical research with several organisations and real-life case studies to convince the sceptic in you.

Whether you have started your social media programme or are just thinking about it, the book provides supportive guidelines for promoting employee participation so that social media is not just marketing's job, but the responsibility of all employees. Employee participation here refers to engaging employees in social media activities such as blogging, exchanging ideas through online platforms and co-creation initiatives with customers that require your organisation's experts [knowledge workers] to engage with suppliers, partners, customers – and each other.

The guidelines in this book are based on previous research undertaken in 2012 as part of my MBA at Henley Business School. I conducted my research through interviews with social media professionals in seven highly successful corporations. A further survey was conducted with thirty-nine professionals across the globe in order to generalise the experience of those interviewed. I recently updated my findings through more discussions with social media managers and other advisors, as well as collecting case studies of employee participation in social media. I have referred to the 2012 case studies in this book and included full case studies based on four more interviews conducted between July and September 2015.

This book offers some great insights for social media managers tasked with leading or supporting social media programmes, whether you are an internal agent or a consultant. The book provides a three-step framework for promoting and sustaining employee participation. You will benefit from this book if:

- You are a manager or executive with reservations about how social media could benefit your organisation

- You are a social media manager new to an organisation or to the role

- You manage social communities for your organisation and are finding it difficult to get employees to participate

- You are a team leader who has a passion for social media but you are struggling to get your team members to participate

- You have a social business idea but are not sure how to present it to your boss and ultimately to your organisation

- You are a manager who thinks social media might help your organisation but you would like more real life examples and some empirical evidence.

What Is In This Book?

Many books on social media tell you the *how* in the *what*. This *Smart Sceptic's Guide* tells you the *how* and the *who*.

This book is a B2B social media guide divided into four parts which provide research, tips and insightful interviews describing the essence of an employee participation framework. Part 1 describes the organisational setting in which the learning and change required for social media participation is likely to thrive. It is a mix of academic theory and practitioner experiences. In essence, it argues for the importance of considering your organisation's prevailing culture and organisational environment when planning a change that requires participation. Does the organisation provide an environment that encourages and empowers employees to participate? Do you learn quickly and pivot when you need to? This book will improve your likelihood of success.

Parts 2 to 4 of this book focus on a proposed process for promoting employee participation during social media programmes:

- Affirmation

- Analysis

- Action

Each part starts with a summary of the key takeaways in the section, a discussion of theoretical evidence backing the idea and practical observations based on interviews and surveys conducted as part of the research. The end of each part contains real life case studies for reference and for generating ideas connected to the main idea in the individual sections. The case studies have been provided by social media managers, change leaders and other advisors in small and large corporations that have been involved in supporting and implementing the change needed for employee participation.

Part 2 – Step One: Affirm Your Employees – this section explains the importance of affirmation at the beginning and throughout the change management process. I offer suggestions of how senior management might lead by example and provide visible support for the change. I also cover the important issue of policies and guidelines governing social media as well as ensuring the objective of venturing into social media is clearly communicated to employees.

Part 3 – Step Two: Do Analysis Right focuses on how a social media manager could get the organisation ready for social media change, embark on gathering evidence for 'current state', and then draw a map of where the organisation wants to go – the 'desired state'. I outline a process of understanding the true requirements of the business along with a means of targeting those employees or teams who could act as pioneers for leading the change.

Part 4 – Step Three: Move Into Action describes how employees might move to act. Following analysis, some social media managers reported a tendency for the organisation to remain stuck in analysis, a kind of 'analysis paralyses'. This part provides tips for moving into action and sustaining participation long term, even after the leader and change team is gone.

At the end of this book, I provide access to a survey tool that social media managers could use to gauge participation in their organisation or to identify where there might be gaps, e.g. is there a gap in affirmation or haven't we done enough analysis? It is always worthwhile to benchmark your organisation at the start of your social media effort and then review six, twelve and eighteen months down the line. Is participation sustained? What more needs to be done? It is also important to tie your social media efforts to the impact on the business as part of your measurement tools. This book has some ideas on how this might be done.

Why You Should Read This Book

Often, academic work is difficult to understand and apply in industry. Writing this book has been about translating academic insight on social media into applicable and easy-to-follow actions to benefit managers and executives in business-to-business organisations.

In my eleven-year career, I have undertaken engineering, business development, and in the past five years, senior marketing roles in organisations such as Schlumberger and General Electric. I now work at LR Senergy leading the software marketing strategy, and I am also a part time doctorate student at Strathclyde Business School, Glasgow, UK. My research is in its early stages and focusses on innovative outcomes in big data projects.

As a social media for business enthusiast, I see a gap in social media education addressing corporations still sceptical about venturing into social media and how they might promote employee participation. While the idea of social media for business and employee advocacy has taken off for many companies, particularly those in the Technology space (think IBM, Dell, Google, and Cisco), there are still untapped opportunities across other sectors, such as energy, publishing, manufacturing and the likes.

If you're looking for information on *how* to use social technology and platforms, e.g. Twitter, Pinterest, LinkedIn, there is a lot out there. But there aren't enough guidelines for managers and executives, newly appointed social media managers and online community managers on how to stimulate, encourage and sustain participation in social media programmes. Such programmes are critical because they promote brand awareness, influence a firm's reputation and establish the organisation and its employees as thought leaders. They also enable collaboration and other performance enhancing measures. I have always been curious about why some organisations can take a new idea or technology and get employees excited about it, becoming ambassadors as they collaborate inside and outside their organisations, while other organisations (or specific teams within organisations) struggle with employee participation.

INTRODUCTION

Social Media For Business

Technology based organisations have been the most progressive in adopting social technologies (Bradley & McDonald, 2011; Bughin, Byers, & Chui, 2011; Owyang, Jones, Tran, & Nguyen, 2011). The application of social technologies include co-creation projects, blogging platforms, content communities, customer service via social networking sites and virtual worlds, e.g. gaming. These tech organisations have managed the change process with reasonable success, stimulating significant employee participation in their organisations. The change appears to be embedded with a heavy learning process that over time, evolves within the organisation. Therefore, an organisation is not successful because of new or fancy technology. It is successful because it has cultivated an environment where employees are empowered to participate actively in social media initiatives (Shirky, 2011).

1

Consciously changing and learning often results in a virtuous participation process. But first, why all the interest in social organisations and what must organisations be able to do to achieve participation? Rather than leave social media initiatives to the marketing function, achieving company-wide participation can have a powerful impact on brand image and customer engagement. It is this process that I focus on in this book, with the support of research and real life case studies.

Organisations used to be able to control brand perceptions through press releases and good PR. This enabled organisations to tell customers what to think about their products and services. But as a result of social media, some argue that organisations have been increasingly relegated to mere observers, not having the knowledge, chance or even right in some cases to alter publicly posted comments by customers. Wikipedia, for example, forbids the participation of firms in its online community.

Kaplan & Haenlein (2010) define social media as:

A group of Internet-based applications that build on the ideological and technological foundations of Web 2.0 [web application that allows participatory information sharing and collaboration], and that allow the creation and exchange of user-generated content.

As social media comes to the top of many corporations' agendas, terms such as 'social organisation' and 'social business' have been coined to describe organisations that lead in social participation and collaboration internally and externally with customers, collaborators and suppliers. Becoming a social organisation or business means enabling mass collaboration, where social media is one of the key avenues to enablement, not the end itself. Bradley and McDonald (2011) suggest that in a social organisation, employee collaboration and participation is applied strategically to create value by addressing significant business challenges and opportunities.

Social media change cannot be embarked on light-heartedly. It involves various levels of realignment of roles, structures, policies and processes (Owyang, Jones, Tran, & Nguyen, 2011). A 2011 survey by Strategy& (the strategy consulting group in PwC) (Premo & Vollmer, 2011) reveals that the 'ability to adapt and react quickly' is the most important success factor for social media implementation. Like many new technologies – particularly in a digital age – social media change needs to be supported by a cultural transformation within the organisation in a way that enables flexibility, adaptability and fast learning. Being social has to be in the lifeblood of the organisation, or the organisation has to be willing to acquire social capabilities and make those a core competence. In the next chapter, I examine the role of organisational environments in promoting social business characteristics.

FIGURE 1: SOCIAL MEDIA SUCCESS FACTORS
(PREMO & VOLLMER, 2011)

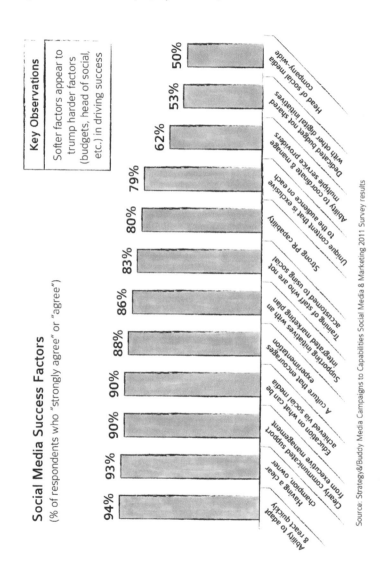

Key Observations

Softer factors appear to trump harder factors (budgets, head of social, etc.) in driving success

Social Media Success Factors
(% of respondents who "strongly agree" or "agree")

Factor	%
Ability to adapt & react quickly	94%
Having a clear champion, owner	93%
Clearly communicated support from executive management	90%
Education on what can be achieved via social media	90%
A culture that encourages experimentation	88%
Supporting initiatives with an integrated marketing plan	86%
Training of staff who are not accustomed to using social	83%
Strong PR capability	80%
Unique content that is exclusive to the audience on each	79%
Ability to coordinate & manage multiple service providers	62%
Dedicated budget not shared with other digital initiatives	53%
Head of social media company-wide	50%

Source: Strategy&/Buddy Media Campaigns to Capabilities Social Media & Marketing 2011 Survey results

PART 1 – ORGANISATION ENVIRONMENT MATTERS

An organization's ability to learn, and translate that learning into action rapidly, is the ultimate competitive advantage.

Jack Welch

Part 1 Highlights

- Employees can participate through blogging, virtual worlds, and collaborative projects

- Employees' behaviour should be the target for the change. Changing their attitude comes later

- A learning environment enables change and promotes sustainable participation

- The characteristics of a learning environment are similar to critical success enablers for social media

- Social media change is incremental, made up of small but frequent improvements over time

- Participation in social media could improve organisational performance through brand perception and brand trust that ultimately impact the bottom line.

1. YOU WANT YOUR EMPLOYEES TO PARTICIPATE

When some organisations hear the words 'employee participation' they get excited about the possibilities that could bring for the organisation. It could mean that the organisation's very best experts are interacting with customers regularly and using thought leadership to build credibility for their products and services. It could generate goodwill that leads to more sales. Many organisations, however, hear 'employee participation' and get concerned. How will we control what employees do?

Let's start by explaining what I mean by participation.

Glew, O'Leary-Kelly & Van Fleet define participation in their 1995 *Journal of Management* paper called, 'Participation in Organizations: A Preview of the Issues and Proposed Framework for Future Analysis':

The essence of participation is a conscious and intended effort by individuals at a higher level in an organization to provide visible extra role or role-expanding opportunities for individuals or groups at a lower level in the organization to have a greater voice in one or more areas of organizational performance.

Based on this definition, participation is about giving employees a greater voice and more stake in the organisation's performance. In this instance, the stake is in social media and helping the organisation reach target performance by sharing knowledge socially, internally and externally.

I mentioned some types of social applications earlier in this book. Let's look at some of the different purposes of social applications:

- **Co-creation projects** enable joint simultaneous creation of content by many end-users, including customers. They allow community-based collection and the rating of content or idea. The main objective of this type of collaboration is that the joint effort between buyer [the customer] and supplier [the organisation] leads to better outcomes in the form of better products and services, enhanced processes and increased technology adoption by the customer. For instance, Ideastorm was launched by Dell in 2007. It has thousands of ideas submitted to its website www.ideastorm.com. As at May 2015, Dell had implemented over 550 ideas out of the nearly 25,000 ideas submitted by customers, partners and other audiences. Employees regularly join and facilitate conversations and 'storm sessions'. If Dell employees did not participate, Ideastorm would be a hole where stuff might go in but nothing would come out.

• **Blogging** represents the earliest form of social media. They are usually managed by one person; others may participate by adding comments. For example, the CEO of Sun Micro-systems maintained a personal blog to improve the transparency of his company. Many organisations have blogs, often launched from their main website. Check out the websites and associated blogs of IBM, SAP, Oracle, Hewlett Packard and General Electric. Other organisations with prolific blogs are Disney, Allstate and ADP. All these blogs are kept fresh with engaging content by employees.

- **Content communities** allow the sharing of media content between users. Such external communities include YouTube, while some organisations have their own internal communities. Although such communities carry inherent risks, e.g. employees sharing copyrighted materials, these communities are an attractive contact channel for many organisations. Cisco and Google use such communities to share recruiting videos, keynotes, speeches and press announcements, both internally and externally. In recent times, employees can share employer branded content with in such communities, usually through a controlled platform.

- **Social networking sites** are very popular among many organisations. External sites (e.g. LinkedIn, Twitter and Facebook) enable users to connect by creating personal profiles and inviting friends and colleagues to access them. Such sites may be used to access product reviews and information or to provide expert support to customers. Some organisations such as Dell (follow @DellCares) and JetBlue Airways (follow @JetBlue) use Twitter as a customer service channel.

- **Virtual worlds** can be gaming, e.g. Second Life or Foursquare. They are used in advertising and communication. For instance, organisations that have participated in Second Life include massively multiplayer online role-playing games (MMORPG), or social worlds such as SIBM, Cisco and Microsoft (Barnetta, 2009).

Social media programmes that require employees to promote their organisations as part of their role are called Employee Advocacy programmes[1]. Such systems cannot be successful unless employees participate! Recent research proves employees' participation in the digital world generates significant advantages to sales, business development, thought leadership, brand loyalty and employee engagement and retention. Daniel Hebert (2015), Digital Marketing Manager at an Employee Advocacy software company, PostBeyond[2], provides some indications in his LinkedIn Post:

- Sales reps using social media as part of their sales techniques outsell 78% of their peers[3]

---

1   Source from http://whatis.techtarget.com/definition/employee-advocacy

2   Check out the company website at www.postbeyond.com

3   Source: http://www.forbes.com/sites/markfidelman/2013/05/19/study-78-of-salespeople-using-social-media-outsell-their-peers/

- 72.6% of salespeople using social selling as part of their sales process outperformed their sales peers and exceeded quota 23% more often[4]

- 77% of B2B buyers said they did not talk with a salesperson until after they had performed independent research[5]

- 92% of buyers say they delete emails or voicemail messages from someone that they do not know[6]

- Content shared by employees receives eight times more engagement than content shared by brand channels[7]

- Only 33% of buyers trust the brand whilst 90% of customers trust product or service recommendations from people they know[8]

- Employees of socially engaged companies are[9]:
  - 57% more likely to align social media engagement to more sales leads

4   Source: https://www.slideshare.net/secret/kFdU767zyWS30G

5   Source: http://www.executiveboard.com/

6   Source: https://www.slideshare.net/secret/211obqeB5hMVql

7   Source: http://www.socialmediatoday.com/content/employee-advocate-mobilize-your-team-share-your-brand-content

8   Source: Nielsen Global Online Consumer Survey

9   Source: http://www.altimetergroup.com/2014/10/relationship-economics-linkedin/

- 20% more likely to stay at their company
- 27% more likely to feel optimistic about their company's future
- 40% more likely to believe their company is more competitive.

So how does an organisation promote employee participation on these or similar platforms? Let's look at participatory change, i.e. an organisational change, which requires the participation of employees to be successful and sustainable.

Possibly the most effective way of developing a habit in our daily life, e.g. exercising, is to be shaped by the desired recurring patterns of behaviour. One's knowledge, attitude and belief must be targeted in order to change behaviour. It is similar in the case of participatory change. Several scholars note that targeting behaviour during participatory change enforces the desired patterns of behaviour, and more importantly makes the change sustainable (Beer, Eisenstat, & Spector, 1990; Kotter & Cohen, 2002; Balogun & Hope-Hailey, 2004). When highlighting the benefits of employee participation, other scholars have noted that participation could develop a powerful foundation for extensive learning in the organisation (O'Keeffe, 2002). This helps avoid mediocrity and alleviates the problem of lack of commitment (de Caluwe & Vermaak, 2004a).

However, even in daily life people are more likely to change behaviour if they are shown a truth that influences them such that they make an emotional connection with the new behaviour. The new behaviour essentially causes a fundamental shift in attitude.

The outcome of participatory change could be unpredictable, and is perhaps the basis of the concerns that some organisations have about allowing employees to participate in social media. But unpredictability is not always detrimental. The direction and magnitude of unpredictability depends significantly on the learning ability of employees and the effectiveness of the learning environment itself. Get those two elements right and employee participation is likely to have a positive lasting impact on organisational performance.

2. WHAT A LEARNING ENVIRONMENT DOES FOR PARTICIPATION

One way to know if your organisation has a conducive learning environment is whether it has embedded learning processes within its structure. These processes will be present across functions and projects alike, and will enable enhanced organisational capacity to change or transform more quickly than an organisation which doesn't have them. Peter Senge, renowned for his work on learning organisations, defines such environments as places where employees continually expand their capacity to create desirable results, where their new ideas are nurtured and collective aspiration is set free (Senge, 1990). I would go even further and say that a learning environment is one where failure is not feared but is celebrated. After all, every failing is new knowledge about what does not work.

Key terms used by academics and practitioners, such as Watkins & Marsick, 1993; Doppler (2004); and Owyang, Jones, Tran, & Nguyen, 2011, to describe the elements of an environment that make it conducive to learn, create and change are:

- Shared vision

- Team learning (an accumulation of individual learning)

- Diverse cross-functional teams

- Training

- Dedicated resources

- Calculated experimentation

- A culture of feedback.

This is not an exhaustive list, but the idea is there. If an organisation can establish a majority of these traits within its environment, it's more likely to promote an environment that enables learning and ultimately realises the required change.

Some research has found positive links between these elements and employee participation – not necessarily in the context of social media specifically, but a similar idea could apply. It is not farfetched to suggest that if employees feel empowered through a learning environment, they are likely to participate in the activities in that environment.

When I examine the characteristics of a learning environment and put them next to the success enablers for social media as postulated by practitioners in the field, the similarities are stark. Take a look at the table below.

TABLE 1: SOCIAL MEDIA SUCCESS ENABLERS AND LEARNING ENVIRONMENT CHARACTERISTICS

Social media critical success enablers according to study by Strategy& (the strategy consulting group in PwC)	Characteristics of a learning environment by numerous researchers dating back to 1990
Adapt and react quickly	Experimentation
Experimentation	Open communication
Clearly communicated support	Teams
Training	Training
Clear champion	Resources
Culture	Culture of feedback

This book is not intended to help organisations build a learning environment but to provide a guide as to what to gauge your organisation with. As a leader or manager considering participation in social media programmes, start off with exploring the current environment to understand how to influence existing norms about learning and change. Is the environment conducive for learning? Can it get people to participate in its current state?

During my interviews with social media change agents, six qualities emerged as most important for employee participation to thrive.

- A willingness and ability to experiment

- Training and support for employees

- A shared vision

- Open and clear communication

- A collaborative environment

- Trust.

One social media manager at a successful technology company noted, 'I think it's important to have an organisation that encourages open communication and focuses on a collaborative and innovative culture for employees.' This message was recurring in the majority of interviews and in the survey that I later administered to thirty-nine social media professionals globally.

However, I should note that simply because an organisation has a learning environment does not mean that employees will definitely participate in social media programmes. And the reverse is true – just because an organisation finds a way to generate and enforce employee participation is not an indication that it has a learning environment. What I am suggesting is that the similarities between characteristics of such an environment and the enablers of *sustainable* employee participation in social programmes cannot be ignored. It is therefore incredibly helpful if learning effectively and continuously is already in the lifeblood of your organisation.

3. THE CHANGE MANAGEMENT PROCESS

Social media is new technology in the workplace. Therefore, the change management process associated with incorporating social media programmes into the day to day practices of an organisation would resemble the change process that comes with introducing any new technology in the workplace, e.g. a new ERP system. To a great extent, the severity of the change depends on how great a cultural shift it is for each organisation. I found through research that nearly half of the organisations I engaged with felt that social media was a natural extension of the way they previously worked.

Some organisations may have existing systems and processes that could be adapted to suit the purposes of social media programmes. For others, the change may be more dramatic, requiring a series of technical, cultural and behavioural reconstruction (Balogun & Hope-Hailey,

2004). In this book, I do not cover technical changes such as introduction of new systems and platforms. I will continue to focus on how to make behavioural changes that result in active employee participation (Bradley & McDonald, 2011).

To embed and sustain the desired culture, the attitude of employees needs to change after behaviour changes (Balogun & Hope-Hailey, 2004). Employees need to understand and value what is being achieved. The new way of doing things has to make sense to them (Kotter & Cohen, 2002). Efforts to change attitude (or values) before behaviour could mean that employees – with changed attitudes – find themselves working in a system that does not support their new attitudes (Balogun & Hope-Hailey, 2004). Values have to be rooted in day-to-day practice. Hence, behaviour should change first before a new attitude can become a reality (Hendry, 1996).

Researchers suggest that most transformational changes occur longer-term through an evolutionary path. The term evolutionary change stems from Charles Darwin's work in biology, but can be used to describe a type of change in organisations that is gradual and happens over time without a clear end point. Researchers like Wang & Ahmed (2003) also suggest that incremental changes may only provide a temporary change that doesn't make the long haul, and that through continuous organisational learning, an organisation might deliver value and sustainable competitive advantage. This doesn't necessarily mean that incremental change doesn't have a role in organisations or that it is unimportant. What this implies is that today's fast-paced environment requires continuous breakthrough changes to combat the ever-changing face of social interactions.

Richard Luecke's work in *Managing Change and Transitions* (2003) describes continuous incremental change as a series of small but frequent improvements. This notion is supported by Susan Emerick, formerly Senior Social Business Director at IBM in a 2012 interview I conducted. She notes: 'It was an evolving process where we were constantly experimenting with possible approaches, then applying insights from what's working or not working and then iterating to enhance what's working to make it even better.'

FIGURE 2: CONTINUOUS, FREQUENT IMPROVEMENTS

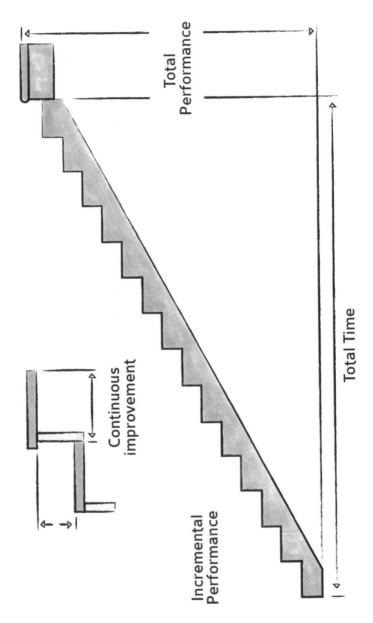

Based on my research, changes associated with technological implementations constitute a continuous process
rather than an event with an end point, after which
the organisation can expect to return to a reasonably
steady state. It appears that the changes which organisations need to make while implementing social media
programmes cannot all be anticipated ahead of time
(Orlikowski & Hofman, 1997).

Dell's social media journey is an example of how change
is an incremental process of small but frequent steps
towards social media mastery. In 2006, Dell started a
series of small, frequent improvements and experiments
in social media, including the implementation of internal and external blogs, and training that finally led to it
being named the #1 social brand.

In 2011, Jeremiah Owyang and his team investigated
several companies such as IBM and Intel and their
'social business readiness'. The result of the study is a
'social business hierarchy of needs' model comprising
of incremental stages: foundation, safety, formation,
enablement and enlightenment stages. These stages
resemble a series of small but crucial steps that lead to
'enablement', a stage that appears to be transformational

so that it leads to 'enlightenment', a foundational change to the psyche of an organisation (Owyang, Jones, Tran, & Nguyen, 2011).

4. INSIGHT:
THE FIFTH BUSINESS

Interview With Enda Logan, CEO at The Fifth Business and Visiting Professor at Robert Gordon University, Aberdeen, Scotland

Date of Interview: 11 September 2015

About The Fifth Business

Committed to systematically improving technology exploitation through better engagement techniques, Enda Logan and Joan Ingram set up The Fifth Business in 1994, developing it into a leading change communications, training, multimedia and virtual working consultancy. Nowadays, the company generates revenues of around US$20million annually and has offices in London, Houston, Aberdeen and The Hague with seventy-five full-time consulting, media and training staff whose projects have taken them to every continent.

The Fifth Business started out working mainly with oil and gas majors (e.g. BP, Marathon, ConocoPhillips, ExxonMobil and Shell) before expanding its client base to healthcare, construction, pharma, manufacturing, finance and energy-related firms. Focusing on internal audiences, The Fifth Business facilitates the change process within companies, usually triggered by establishing **obligatory** regulatory processes, such as those for health, safety, environment and quality in the workplace, and implementation of a new or modified **strategic** direction or the introduction of new **technology,** e.g. social media.

Although The Fifth Business dabbles in PR, it usually serves an internal purpose within a company. Enda admits that The Fifth Business is becoming increasing fixated with change and the management of it. He ponders: 'How do you get a population of people to want to go somewhere, ensure they are aware of why they are going there, that they are armed with the skills they need to achieve the objective and get them to be productive in the new end state?'

During his interview, Enda tackles aspects of this puzzle in regards to change management in organisations.

Key Elements Of Changing Behaviours

In obligatory change, a firm will need to show compliance such that every employee changes as a matter of regulation, regardless of current business environment and performance. More and more, firms need to think about how to persuade people to change behaviour even when it's clearly in their best interest. Enda uses the example of smoking, noting that most smokers know smoking is harmful to them but they do it anyway. How can we communicate to these people in such a way that they want to stop smoking?

In strategic change, Enda observes that most managers become isolated from the rest of the workforce and often send out intentions for strategic change via a memo. Ultimately, many organisations communicate change from the top down – that is the typical hierarchy of communication. Enda notes that this is an inverted model, and that firms should rather think about what is in it for the employee.

He illustrates with an example:

SAP, a new software that could provide significant performance advancement for a company, will likely increase workload for the employee on the shop floor.

The employee now needs to learn a new tool and enter data into a new system. Enda explains that firms need to speak in the language of the employee by communicating the gains SAP will provide long term – gains that the employee will care about. Enda remarks, '"Thou shall use SAP" is just not sufficient.'

In technology change – specifically social media – Enda believes that there is an evolution going on, not just in organisations but also in society, where very powerfully, but subtly, things are changing. Gone are the days that things said inside a firm stay inside the firm. Today, firms need to make sure that whatever is said in a communiqué inside the firm is written in such a way that it can appear on the front page of a newspaper – or indeed on social media.

The rules of the game have changed. Enda tells his customers to be very subtle about how they use social media to avoid coming across as a corporate voice. He advises companies to experiment using employees who exemplify the companies' brand and have them participate on social media. Rather than having a corporate voice, a firm can have ambassadors speaking on social media about what they are doing and what they know – and by the way, they work for Company X. Enda explains that this approach, kept relevant, could be very powerful to a company's brand.

What's Corporate Culture Got To Do With It?

When asked to describe a 'smart organisation' with the ideal corporate culture successful in social media, Enda notes that a smart organisation doesn't allow its business's consequence and power to reside in the IT department, but rather takes ownership across the business. Smart organisations think about what's working and what isn't, possibly using tools such as root cause analysis to determine success and failure factors. Such organisations – once they have identified what works – make plans to replicate this approach throughout the company. In the same vein, such organisations identify what doesn't work and eradicate it.

Enda tells a story of a man he once met whose job title was Corporate Jester

He worked with an airline company and his job was to sit in all the company's board meetings and question what people said, but not without cause. He was paid to 'say the unsayable' and challenge things that very senior executives and board members were suggesting. Clearly an enlightened board that wanted a different perspective on things, this kind of organisation visibly encourages a probing, questioning mentality. Enda describes this organisation as a smart one, explaining, 'Having systematised objectivity, such an organisation has the capacity to step outside itself and critically observe.'

Ultimately, full-throated participation requires employees to share their knowledge – knowledge that employees regard as power. Why would they want to relinquish that power? The culture of a firm must be one that provides an environment where employees can see value in sharing their knowledge.

Becoming A Smart Company

Enda's advice to companies wanting to develop 'smart' characteristics in their organisational environment is that senior leadership should first be seen to 'live' the values they want employees to adopt. He emphasises that he doesn't mean playing lip service – putting up attractive posters or pictures of the Grand Canyon with the word

'Vision' beneath. He is referring to leaders who actively model the desired behaviour. That's a good start. He notes, 'Change always starts at the top'.

He further notes that as part of employees' development and engagement, companies should expect that employees will spend some time on social media, building networks, gaining and sharing knowledge with customers and stakeholders. Companies can leverage the power and engagement derived from employee participation so that it is beneficial to the business.

Enda advises companies to equip employees with better technology platforms for collaboration and co-creation, e.g. SharePoint, blogging and so on. Use online training or face-to-face – whatever kind of training is available – so that employees are constantly kept up-to-date with the latest technology and skills.

And finally on being 'smart', Enda notes that the capacity to change is crucial on one hand, but companies also need to be able to change repeatedly as a deliberate future-proofing strategy.

Sustainable Change: A Tricky Tension

There appears to be a delicate balance between making change stick in such a way that employees do not go back to how things used to be after a period and the ability to be able to change again when environment or market forces require it. How do companies ensure that change is sticky but still possess the capacity to change again?

Enda says, 'Trust but verify.'

Collect lessons learned of what works and what doesn't. He also encourages companies to tell stories, ensuring that people are aware of the good things happening as a result of the new behaviour. At the same time, there needs to be operational processes that monitor the organisation so that employees do not revert to familiar, comfortable practices.

Enda refers to Martin Seligman's 'Learned Helplessness' theory when discussing some of the issues with change in organisation. He explains, using the example of helpdesks, 'If people know that there's a helpdesk, they will not try to fix the problem themselves.'

He notes that the structure of helpdesks is changing for the better now, but that for years, helpdesks were simply logging printer problems. Enda explains that changing is not about logging a problem. It is about seeking the source of the problem, which could be education, training or awareness, and addressing it with intervention. Enda shares a real life experience about the time one of his staff flew to a location to solve a PC problem that had been going on at a customer's site for weeks, saying, 'When my guy arrived there, it turned out the problem was that the senior manager hadn't plugged the thing into the wall!'

What companies need to avoid is the development of learned helplessness, where employees become familiar with an undesired behaviour that has been going for a long time and simply follow that behavioural pattern.

Enda provides an antithesis: 'When introducing new technology, train some people in behaviours around the technology, allowing them to model others' approach, so that, as much as possible, the employees' first experience of the new technology is positive.'

Enda explains that many times people walk away from technology physically and mentally merely because it didn't work the first time. These trained employees can now model a culture within their organisation that promotes change and makes it stick.

How can an organisation develop the ability to change again though? Enda observes,

'As Scotland's national bard, Robert Burns, has observed, one of the greatest gifts is being able to step outside of yourself and see yourself the way others see you. It could completely change the way you feel about yourself.'

At the end of any project, companies need to debrief in a structured way, clearly identifying and sharing what they did, what worked really well and what didn't work so well.

Companies should give people permission to speak freely about such things, and not in a politically-charged environment where their career might be at stake. Captured lessons should be referenced in future projects. That way companies pass the torch of knowledge on by word of mouth, taking into consideration the human element of change.

These lessons can help develop a systematised way of learning and changing in an organisation.

About Enda @ The Fifth Business and Robert Gordon University

Before founding The Fifth Business in 1994, Enda worked in a variety of broadcasting (BBC) and senior management roles in training and marketing disciplines in the oil and gas industry. In 2014, he was appointed Visiting Professor at the Robert Gordon University, Aberdeen in association with the school's undergraduate and postgraduate communications and public relations programmes. He is personally passionate about data visualisation. Enda comes from Northern Ireland but lives in Aberdeen, Scotland from where he travels extensively for work assignments and business development.

In this section, reflect on:

- Does your organisation encourage learning, changing and effective feedback?

- How different is the current culture compared to a culture that would thrive on being social?

- To what extent does your organisation encourage failure and experimentation and put processes in place to learn from them?

PART 2– STEP 1: AFFIRM YOUR EMPLOYEES

An affirmation opens the door. It's a beginning point on the path to change

Louise L. Hay

Part 2 highlights:

- It's a great start if the CEO participates on social media. It empowers employees to do the same

- CEO participation alone is insufficient. Middle management layers need to support the change

- Make the social media vision clear to everyone

- Hard wire social media activities to the business's vision for performance and growth

- Don't do social just because everyone else is

- Make the rules clear, simple, easily accessible and repeat them again and again

- Don't reinvent the wheel – there's some great stuff out there already

- Emphasise on what's allowed just as much as (or more than) what is not allowed

- Communicate effectively from the top to the bottom.

5. LEADERS AS EXAMPLES

Corporate initiatives can be a bit like 'do as I say, not as I do'. If you are a parent, you might understand that your children watch you and would rather copy your actions than obey to your admonishments. From a child's perspective, it must be ridiculous to be told to do one thing and find the instructing adult doing the opposite. In the case of social media, employees want to see their leaders engaged and leading the way. Leaders in businesses that preach social business and online interactions with customers, suppliers or whoever else must be seen to walk the talk.

A leader must not only communicate support and commitment but also be engaged in social media in some form. Leaders like CEO of Salesforce.com Marc Benioff have done an outstanding job of being present on social platforms such as Twitter in a way that encourages his employees to follow suit. It's a sign that says, 'Hey, I buy into this!' Over recent years, more reasons have been uncovered as to why CEOs should be social that dispute some of the risks involved in putting one's self out there for scrutiny.

The 2014 Brandfog survey [10] on the Social CEO revealed interesting findings. For instance, the perception that executive participation in social media leads to better leadership had grown from 45% to 75% between 2012 and 2013. Respondents also believed that it built brand trust that could really come in handy during a crisis. For a CEO looking for reasons to participate in social media (rather than reasons not to), here they are: the world will perceive a CEO as more trustworthy if he or she is on social media, plus employees might be motivated to participate in a recently launched social programme.

Still, by the end of 2014, 68% of Fortune 500 CEOs had no social media presence on major platforms such as LinkedIn, Twitter, Facebook or Google+. CEOs like Tim Cook (Apple) and Satya Nadella (Microsoft) are active on Twitter, with Jeff Immelt (General Electric) and Meg Whitman (Hewlett Packard) having more than 100,000 followers on LinkedIn.[11]

---

10 Source from http://brandfog.com/CEOSocialMediaSurvey/
    BRANDfog_2014_CEO_Survey.pdf

11 Source from http://www.adweek.com/socialtimes/social-
    ceo-2014/504035

It is not always possible for the CEO of your organisation to be a social media guru. It doesn't appear to stop employee participation outright if the CEO is not into social media, but it does make the job of a social media or community manager more difficult.

While executive support helps, one global social media manager at a top social brand noted to me that it was more important to have a layer of middle and senior managers that support and engage in the change. Depending on the level in the organisation which a social media manager is trying to influence, the CEO might be just too far away to be an effective role model. The CEO's participation could mean little to the guy on the shop floor who could be valuable as a thought leader on a corporate product co-creation blog.

Throughout my research, I found that senior managers reinforced values by talking about them and behaving in ways that supported them. Employees were empowered by this. And with the right guidelines (I'll touch on this later), employees began to participate. There was a reasonably strong relationship between the affirmation that employees got and the level of active participation that resulted in the organisation.

6. CLARIFY THE VISION, STATE THE RULES

Many organisations get worked up about what the rules should be, and rightly so! We have read about social media disasters, and the debate goes on about whether companies can truly control what employees do and say on social media. If employee participation is to improve an organisation's performance, then the vision needs to be clear to employees. As a manager, you will need to state and echo the rules again and again.

Major corporations encouraging social media participation have in-depth information on their website on participation guidelines, such as what not to do or say, the language to use and where to go if an employee is not sure. It is generally an open approach with such companies that focusses on what is allowed rather than what is prohibited. Intel, for instance, have a great site for employee social media guidelines. I referred to it a fair bit when developing guidelines with a previous employer. I love Intel's three rules of engagement: 'Disclose, Protect, Use Common Sense'[12]. They are simple, encouraging and repeatable. They don't have lots of sentences beginning with *do not*. And most importantly, they tell Intel employees what to do if they screw up.

Another great example of an organisation with clear guidelines is Hewlett Packard (HP). The organisation's blogging code of conduct is easily accessible and is linked to its Standard of Business Conduct so it's pretty joined up with its overall vision. It also includes some moderation. For instance, the guidelines note that comments will be reviewed before being posted on the corporate blog[13].

TIP

If you are looking to create guidelines in your role, I suggest you have a look at Intel's site as well as HP's and Dell's. Borrow what works for your organisation and modify as necessary. You don't need to reinvent the wheel.

The potential for something to go wrong in social media shouldn't deter organisations aspiring to be social

---

12 Source from http://www.intel.com/content/www/us/en/legal/intel-social-media-guidelines.html

13 Source from http://www.hp.com/hpinfo/blogs/codeofconduct.html

businesses. If you have got this far into this book, you might be thinking the same. There are real benefits for your brand in being a social organisation. You'll not just establish your organisation as a thought leader, collaborative and genuinely interested in what customers want, but also you'll benefit when it comes to recruitment and managing a crisis if you already have some kind of online presence.

It is not uncommon for large organisations to encounter a social media crisis now and again, hence there is significant existing information about how to manage such crises. For instance, the Social Media Examiner wrote a blog post using case studies to illustrate how brands might defend their reputation online[14].

Crises may happen, but that is where your clear guidelines on managing a crisis come in. Like Intel and HP, every organisation should have some.

Now let's assume you have weighed the pros and cons of being social and you have decided it is a good idea to get involved. Don't get into social media simply because other companies like yours are doing it. All my interviews with social media change agents led to the same conclusion on this:

---

14 Source from http://www.socialmediaexaminer.com/defend-your-social-media-reputation/

You have to link the purpose of social media to agreed business objectives from the onset.

What is the business trying to achieve? Is it X% more sales from a specific segment of the market? Is it to generate X number of products for a new market? Is it to retain the loyalty of a group of customers likely to be lured by a new player in the market? Any social media programme will need to show early results that enable the business to achieve its vision. This becomes key in gaining commitment from senior management.

Senior managers want to see goals hard wired to the purpose of the social media programme(s), particularly if it requires investment, allocated resources and the time of employees who could easily be working on something else. Any manager with this responsibility will need to sell the cause and make a business case. This will be easy if you've had the business's goals on your mind from the start.

7. COMMUNICATE SUPPORT FROM THE TOP

Effective communication is needed for employees to understand the vision clearly and be inspired by it. Prof Rosabeth Moss Kanter in her 2005 Harvard Business Review article, 'Leadership for Change: Enduring Skills for Change Masters', notes that 'there is a gap between dreaming and doing that is filled by the support of others'. She also notes employees need to be supported in the move from 'dreaming' to 'doing' through role modelling and walking the talk. Clearly communicating support, not just from executive levels but from direct managers [middle managers, shop managers, team leaders], is key in enabling a drive to participation.

While active participation could be ideal for mass engagement and business impact, researchers like Armenakis, Harris, & Mossholder (1993) observe that this kind of participation may hamper clear, effective communication. Some researchers recommend a top-down dissemination of information to employees: a 'telling and selling' approach that ensures information does not get diluted as it is passed from one employee to another (Russ, 2008). There is often a worry that communication can be less efficient, or even misinterpreted in participatory approaches due to many degrees of translation and iteration of information. Managers must ensure that the nature, scope and reason for the change is communicated repeatedly in a way that employees understand. Effective communication is a two-way street of talking and listening. Therefore, there should be room for employees to give feedback or ask questions where clarification is required.

Many of those interviewed provided interesting ways of ensuring effective and clear communication. Some channels include email, screensavers, posters, videos, blog and commentary, training, online resources, and remote or face-to-face weekly or monthly meetings. There is also consideration for different individuals and how they are likely to search and/or digest information. For instance, a social media manager at SAS, a business analytics software company, notes, 'Not everyone logged on the Intranet so we used emails and other forms of communication to reach them'.

Another social media community manager told me that he did not rely on written communication alone. He verbalised communication through monthly calls with the community.

Eventually, it comes down to how an organisation shows support and communicates change. It makes the change more difficult if the organisation has to change the way it would normally communicate. How an organisation communicates to its employees tends to be wired into the culture. If it is top-down then I advise that managers leverage that. If it is peer-to-peer or via project groups, then use this effectively, keeping in mind that information translation might need to be monitored so that the 'right' information is being shared and interpreted correctly. Use employee surveys, secure discussion forums and scenario quizzes[15] to ascertain whether the message you are sending is being received. This also helps you measure the number of employees receiving and understanding the message. Set up a helpdesk and/or help document so that employees with questions can get answers quickly.

---

15 Source from http://snapcomms.com/solutions/communicating-change-to-employees

8. INSIGHT: BLOCK IMAGING INTERNATIONAL

Interview With Krista Kotrla, Senior Vice President Marketing at Block Imaging International

Date of Interview: 29 July 2015

About Block Imaging

Block Imaging is a medical equipment company that buys and sells diagnostic equipment globally. The company was established in 1997. Block Imaging now has over 100 employees as its culture evolves around its diverse workforce. The company has faced the kinds of challenges that start-ups often face, such as building credibility in the marketplace, hiring the right people and understanding how the company can generate competitive advantage to grow profitably.

Block Imaging didn't start out being social media savvy, but since 2010, the company has transformed into a solid social business and has incorporated a content marketing strategy into its business culture.

Early Marketing Attempts

When Krista Kotrla started with Block Imaging in 2003, there was no social media participation at all. As part of the early marketing efforts, the company attempted to redesign its website. The website still looked like a brochure with equipment lists and little opportunities to interact with customers. The company also went through a phase of buying emailing lists of potential customers. Unfortunately, these didn't lead to the kind of market interaction that Block Imaging had hoped for, nor did they yield significant sales. Instead they increased frustration around the Block Imaging brand.

A Quest To Understand Social Business

Krista also became frustrated, determined to find a way to build credibility for the brand in a different way. She sought to find out how tools like Twitter and LinkedIn might fit Block Imaging's strategy and what the opportunity was for the company to tell their story through such platforms. A key challenge in the medical equipment industry was that companies held information very close to their chest. Also, there were questions about whether anyone from the industry was even on social media.

As a leader, Krista began to research on SEO because she was perplexed as to why the company could spend so much revamping a website but still find that the site did not appear in relevant search engine rankings. During her research, she came across HubSpot[16], a marketing software that helps with blogging, landing pages, emails, subject lines, etc. She notes this in my interview with her:

'Through HubSpot, I could test out a bunch of ideas without it costing thousands of dollars in infrastructure, time and outsourcing.'

Asking For Change

Block Imaging started with a blog. Krista believed this would allow her to experiment, gradually identifying what works and what doesn't.

As with many companies, employees (including management) think potential customers already know the company and what they do.

Krista approached management with ideas of how to use a blog to get found on the Internet for relevant keywords. She helped employees update their LinkedIn profiles, just as she had updated hers. Soon, employees

---

16   Check out http://hubspot.com for more info

were saying, 'Wow! I'm getting connection requests on LinkedIn from people I've never heard of!'

This was probably the first eye-opener for the team. The second eye-opener was when Krista sat in the conference with senior managers and the team, pulled up a Google search page and said, 'What do you wish we showed up for?'

And then she typed in key phrases or words linked to the industry and found Block Imaging was nowhere on the first page, or the second page, or the third page...

The company wasn't showing up. This exercise also applied to key sales executives' names:

'What comes up when people you leave voice messages for Google your name?'

This led to a realisation among the leadership that, ideally, potential customers should find relevant information not just about the company, but about employees as well to provide credibility. Be it a video clip, a how-to blog post or similar, this would increase the chances that a potential customer would call back.

Let's Do This...

The blog eventually started in 2010, with the main goal being to grow customer base through increased web traffic to the website. It was an opportunity to get more visitors to discover Block Imaging as a solution provider when they wanted to buy, sell or use diagnostic imaging equipment.

Senior leaders thought the new blogging idea was great and verbally communicated support. However, only the company's president actually contributed blog content at the beginning. Blogging was an exciting new development that yielded a lot of head nodding, but participation was seen as marketing's responsibility. While marketing did the best they could, they were not technical experts so they needed information from the technical teams in order to put together credible articles and landing pages.

Krista spent a year sitting down with the product experts from time and time to enable the company to build thought leadership online. She would ask them to talk about the products they were working on so that she could address them in the blog posts her team was putting online.

It was a scary thing for the employees (though they knew they had management's support) as they didn't understand how they could post without giving away company secrets. Many employees didn't feel like they were experts to the point that they could write online about the topic. Some sales employees believed their job was to sell and not to write blog posts.

Someone Figured It Out!

Six months into blogging, Krista discovered Marcus Sheridan, owner of The Sales Lion[17], who saved his company from bankruptcy through blogging. He provided six key topics that people are looking for so that the blog posts didn't just attract traffic, they attracted the right kind of traffic.

Krista says, 'This was a real aha moment for me! Someone had finally figured this out.'

---

17 Check out http://thesaleslion.com for more info

These topics were price and cost, product comparisons, best of lists, how-to posts, addressing problems with products transparently and also presenting solutions. These are the things people in buying mode researching options will be typing into Google.

This was pivotal for Krista and Block Imaging. She got affirmation and she could further convince managers and employees to participate in anticipation of the results.

Marcus Sheridan came to Block Imaging for a full day to teach how to develop inbound traffic from blogging, how to build trust and establish a more trusting relationship between the company and the buyer. It shortened the sales cycle because potential customers already saw the company and its employees as thought leaders with several of their questions already answered.

Measure Results Early

Block Imaging used the following metrics to monitor success in their early attempts at blogging:

- Web traffic

- Pages viewed

- Conversion rates via web forms (effectively potential customers handing over their email addresses)

- Number of downloads (for instance, a buyer's guide)

- Number of visitors requesting price.

Block Imaging was effectively growing an emailing list through their blog content – an emailing list that was permission based and consisted of the target audience. The most encouraging aspect for Krista was to see organic traffic growth. Even when updates to the website were done poorly, traffic continued to increase.

Finally, Krista was able to gather management together and say, 'We have proven that blogging increases online traffic, growing our email list and potential buyers!'

She wanted more. She asked management to go all in by asking everyone to participate. There was a kick off training with at least sixty employees (i.e. the number of employees in the company at the time) from all departments, including Accounting and Legal. The company put aside two full days for everyone to participate. This was the event Marcus Sheridan attended and spoke at on the first day. Krista conducted training on the second day to the whole company and she loved watching silos breaking down across teams. All leaders participated in the kick off.

Keeping Up With Participation

Today, the team at Block Imaging hold all-team-meetings where, through storytelling, team members get recognition for good work in front of their colleagues. Storytelling allows Krista to describe what the recipient did and why it was impactful for the company. It instils the message that blogging is still an important part of the company's culture and strategy to grow, connecting with potential customers. It shows other team members in the meeting that it can be that *easy*.

Krista uses storyboarding to build a picture of the journey that a customer goes through so that employees can see how the customer ends up buying a product. She says employees are often amazed, saying things like, 'I knew that customers read my blog article, but I didn't realise they read ninety-eight pages of our website in the first forty-eight hours of discovering us!'

Aside from having her own externally-facing content marketing blog, Krista continues to reaffirm employees, particularly those in sales who find that a potential customer goes quiet after some email interaction. By sending emails with hyperlinks to additional content, Krista can show employees that, though a potential customer has stopped replying, they are clicking on email links and reading content, perhaps to help them convince their own bosses.

Subsequently, the potential customer pops up again after a few weeks, or even months. She says, 'It is validating to see that every interaction has the opportunity to be a resource.'

Krista has moved employees from changing behaviour to changing their attitude. Employees can see the impact of their efforts and now blog because they believe in it.

The team has crafted catchy phrases such as, 'Append before you send', 'Think: link' and 'Question equals content' to help employees remember to provide content whenever possible. This gives potential customers a reason to come back to the company's website.

Here are some stats showing the progress that Block Imaging has made:

TABLE 2: BLOCK IMAGING SOCIAL MEDIA COUNT

Measure	2010	2015
Blogger count	1	60
Web visits per month	7,000	60,000
Confirmed leads per month	10	800
% sales attributed to inbound marketing	5	40

Krista's Last Word On Succeeding

Krista believes that there are a number of ingredients that make social business transformation stick:

- Have a content manager or officer for collecting draft articles that employees submit. The role should be responsible for polishing up and edit posts in the brand voice. They need to be presented in a way that is customer-centric. The role would also ensure SEO for submitted articles.

- Build content production into the normal rituals of the whole company – not just in marketing.

- Include social content generation into the on-boarding process of the company, providing guidelines and starter tips for generating content from the onset of a new job.

- During recruitment of *any* role, seek people who are excited about creating content and identifying themselves as thought leaders in an online business setting.

About Krista @Block Imaging

Krista Kotrla joined Block Imaging as a Marketing Analyst in 2003. She actually applied for a receptionist role six months earlier, but she didn't get it! She is now Senior Vice President of Marketing and continues to inspire a social business culture. She has a personal blog[18] where she provides fantastic posts on content marketing. She can be contacted on Twitter **@KristaKotrla**

18 Check out http://www.kristakotrla.com to access Krista's blog

At the end of Step 1, reflect on:

- Do employees share the same understanding of your social media vision and the guidelines?

- Do employees believe that their leaders support it and walk-the-talk?

- In what way have you attempted to clarify the vision? Has it worked?

- Which channels have you used to communicate your message? Are they working?

- How can you ensure you reach all employees with your message?

PART 3 – STEP 2: DO ANALYSIS RIGHT

When a truth is necessary, the reason for it can be found by analysis, that is, by resolving it into simpler ideas and truths until the primary ones are reached

Gottfried Leibniz

Part 3 highlights:

- Unfreeze your organisation by assessing the present situation and determining your business's requirements

- Participation in planning the change does not seem to be related to the organisation's learning environment

- Participation in planning is strongly linked to active participation in the social media programme when it is eventually launched

- Benchmark current situation with desired directions. If realignment is required, plan it into the change process

- Tie your social programmes' KPIs to the business's goals to make it simpler to show ROI

- Equip employees with tool kits and train them. This saves time and reduces the effort required to take the leap into 'Social'.

9. GET YOUR ORGANISATION READY

Much of change management theory is based on the works of Kurt Lewin (1946). The theory begins on the premise that change targets and the social processes underlying them are relatively stable when the forces driving for change are roughly equal to the forces resisting change (Cummings, 2004). Therefore, a large part of getting an organisation ready for change is to disarm the forces that resist change.

Referring back to Lewin's work, his three-step process of Unfreezing-Moving-Refreezing could help establish sustainable change. Think of it more as a cycle, because after you 'unfreeze' the organisation, you don't stop there. In today's fast-paced environment, and keeping in mind what I have discussed before about continuous change, 'refreezing' will lead to an 'unfreezing' as small, frequent improvements occur in the organisation. Here are the three elements of Lewin's model:

1. Unfreeze the organisation by assessing the present situation. What are the key things that need to be changed in order to achieve the business's goals? Susan Emerick, co-author of *The Most Powerful Brand on Earth* and former social media director at IBM, writes about the first steps in one of her blog articles[19], 'How to Choose an Employee Advocacy Software Technology Partner', where she notes that determining the business's requirements is the very first step. As a manager, you will need to work collaboratively with your team and key stakeholders to determine areas in the business requiring change.

A bid to change might raise the following questions: what are employees' current attitudes and behaviours towards social media? How does the organisation need employees to interact more on with social media compared to the current reality? What key measures need to change? How will employee engagement change it? I have previously mentioned the need to tie social media activity to

---

19 Source from http://susanemerick.com/how-to-choose-a-employee-advocacy-software-technology-partner/

the business's goals. It is the backbone of success, so as you unfreeze your organisation, ensure social media activities and business goals are hard wired together.

2. Moving and making changes in the organisation. I will deal with this more in 'Step Three: Move into Action', but the essence is in making a choreographed transition into social media. The transition timeline needs to be set during the unfreezing planning stage. It is at this stage that listening to employees and engaging with them is invaluable. It appears that social media change begins with early adopters in the organisation who may be in any business unit. They are usually the starting-point of the change because they are influential and passionate about social media. Get these folks on board early on. They will enable the 'Moving' stage actually to move. OK, more on this later.

3. Refreezing the organisation is to do with making changes stick. This is a continuous process of locking and unlocking, but if changes are not permanent, the business's objectives will not be achieved. Social media change does not appear to be a quick change, but one that requires listening, planning

and probing to provide appropriate responses to the internal and external environments. I cover this more in a subsequent chapter.

Many of the change agents I interviewed strongly disagreed that employees were extensively involved in strategic planning and setting guidelines during social media change, so it appears that in reality, organisations are not engaging enough with employees at the planning phases of social media. Researchers like O'Keeffe (2002) suggest that knowledge workers [employees that add value due to their technical skills and are therefore 'experts' in their fields] are more likely to change behaviours if they are involved in discussion and carrying out activities (Armenakis, Harris, & Mossholder, 1993). Characteristics such as engaging employees in planning seem synonymous with a learning environment, but my research showed a weak link between the two. In fact, previous research has shown that high levels of participation do not mean that an organisation is good at learning. There are other factors at play, such as corporate culture, knowledge management capabilities and so on (Thompson & Kahnweiler, 2002). What my research did show was a fairly strong correlation between how many unfreezing activities took place before launching social media programmes and the level of active participation that erupted within the organisation once they were launched.

One social media manager specifically looked at who the target audiences were outside her organisation. She made every effort to understand their goals, the platforms they were on and how they consumed information. This enabled her to design a strategy for employees to participate in the right places in the appropriate way with the target audiences that mattered to her business's goals.

10. BENCHMARK THE STATUS QUO

In order to make any changes, you need to know what the present situation is. You need to diagnose the organisation. This involves revealing the gaps and placing them side by side with the status quo. Compare where you are with where you want to be. Allow continual assessment and improvement in the organisation in a valued direction (Cummings, 2004). For instance, SAS created a social media council in the first place to evaluate and identify gaps in the current organisation. The council stayed in place throughout the change process (Smith, 2009). One question on your mind might be: 'What if the difference between where we are now and where we ought to be is too wide?' The change could take a longer time than initially planned. The misalignment between these two directions could derail any attempt to introduce social programmes, so a realignment needs to be planned for in the change process. There doesn't appear to be a shortcut. Significant executive commitment and stakeholder buy-in is required to support this (Doppler, 2004; Kanter R., 2005).

Participants in my research noted that social media change took anything from three to six years, and could take longer depending on the gaps that a manager discovers in the organisation. Indeed, the road from preparation to a mature process can be varying lengths, and is highly dependent on how big a shift it is for the business. All participants in my research described the beginning of the process as experimental. One consultant noted that the change began with a six-month pilot that provided feedback before the next phase began – a process that was progressing organically. Another example is illustrated by this comment from another social media manager: 'There was no specific deadline for anything. Our social strategy has kind of grown organically over time…We've tried different things…'

As part of your preparation, try things to ascertain what is working and what could work if an alignment is achieved. It should ideally be a flexible iterative process that generates enough data to understand employee behaviour. Data gathered could be:

- Proportion of employees already using social media

- Key social platforms being used, e.g. Twitter, LinkedIn, Pinterest, Facebook, blogs, etc.

- How frequently employees visit such sites

- The job type and rank of those frequenting such sites

- What exactly the goals are of employees that visit these sites

- Whether they are creating content, sharing existing content or simply watching conversations on such sites.

TIP

As a manager, you can compare this to your desired state. For example, are there a group of employees in R&D [Research and Development] that you'd like to advocate for your organisation on customer-facing blogs and perhaps Twitter? If so, are they already on those social media sites? Are you noticing that middle managers in R&D are not using social media? There's your gap.

Identify a few early adopters in the team and have them act as ambassadors, mirroring the desired behaviours to the rest of the team.

11. WHAT WILL WE MEASURE?

Without measurement, a manager has no real evidence of progress or the lack of it. And it's not measuring just anything – it's measuring the right things. As part of preparing for participatory change, many of those I spoke with noted that establishing a way to measure the 'right' things was crucial.

Susan Emerick states, 'We use measurement to optimise on things that are working well and to do less of the things that are not driving results.'

Assuming benchmarks are documented to be used as a reference as the social media programmes progress, you could identify primary measures to be tracked throughout the process of moving into action. The fewer the measures, the better. If the measures are closely knit with the business's goals, even better!

When social business or social advocacy started building momentum a few years ago, there was little to clarify what to measure, what was working, and how it impacted the bottom line for businesses. Social media managers were under pressure to show significant ROI on such programmes and they struggled to do so.

While the pressure to show returns still exists, there is much more insight now into KPIs and how to impact ROI. Particularly since my research, social programmes have credibility as activities that build and drive brand loyalty and trust.

Simple KPI dashboards showing number of blogs posted, follower count[20] and number of views reveal the reach of the social activities. Engagement with customers can easily be measured with metrics such as number of shares, number of comments and likes, and so on.

Internally, employee participation could be measured by number of articles, videos, tweets and such published by teams. The number of employees being trained is key for gauging how the social media message is spreading. For instance, Dell had trained over 5,000 employees in twenty-six countries by 2012, six years after the start of its

---

20 Source from http://www.inc.com/aaron-aders/top-social-media-kpis-in-2013_1.html

social media journey. This helped to embed the culture across the organisation.

If you have set targets for growing participation in specific pockets of the organisation, measure their engagement. Equip them with tool kits to make simpler what might seem like a tremendous task for some employees. For instance, some companies provide 'social media activation' kits in a pre-packaged form to employees during their training. The kit includes examples of tweets, Facebook posts and LinkedIn posts which could get the employees started. It saves employees' time and makes the prospect of becoming active online less daunting.

Managers can measure employees' scale of influence through individual followership, and level of engagement with published content. Increased influence signals that participation is progressing. Find business KPIs to link with this. Is there increased traffic from LinkedIn to your organisation's website? How many of these visits are resulting in sales enquiries and purchases? ROI becomes easier to measure when you can show that overall employee followership on Twitter increased from 50,000 to 500,000 followers just before your organisation's website's Twitter-related traffic increased from 12% to 20%. And let's say out of that 20%, 50% resulted in sales or job enquiries. Great result!

12. INSIGHT: GENERAL ELECTRIC OIL & GAS

Interview With Becky Edwards, Chief Communications Officer at GE Oil & Gas (a division of General Electric)

Date of Interview: 4 September 2015

About GE Oil & Gas

General Electric (GE) is one of the largest industrial companies in the world with over 300,000 employees across eight divisions, which include billion-dollar businesses such as GE Aviation, GE Healthcare, GE Transportation and GE Oil & Gas.

GE has over six million subscribers on YouTube, over a million followers each on LinkedIn and Facebook, and approaching a million on Google+[21]. The company also has significant presence on Instagram and Pinterest.

---

21   Stats checked on ge.com on 12 September 2015

Thousands of GE employees across divisions regularly talk about GE via these social channels. Jeff Immelt, GE's CEO, and Beth Comstock, Vice Chair at GE, are two of the most active and influential personalities on social media channels such as LinkedIn.

It was in the midst of GE's big social media success that GE Oil & Gas began to build and implement a social media presence internally and externally in order to strengthen its brand, attract great talent and engage customers in profitable conversations.

GE Oil & Gas, the face of GE to the oil and gas industry, comprises of several products and services including subsea equipment, the Industrial Internet and measurement-related solutions. It has several offices across the globe, employing over 45,000 employees in eleven locations.

GE Establishes Guidelines

Becky Edwards started her GE journey with social media in her previous role as Global Employee Communications Leader in 2010. GE already had an internal digital social experience, one that was enabling, allowing employees to comment and even retract offensive comments. Becky describes the environment as 'socially-enabling-digitally' and employee-driven. She remembers that at that time, the ability to request a retraction was pretty progressive.

During this time, GE began to re-examine its social media policy as regards employees and their ability to be powerful brand ambassadors externally as well. It raised questions about what employees could say in the name of self-expression. By 2012, GE had put together a robust set of guidelines for external social media activities.

An Experiment With Potential

After being a part of GE for two years, Becky joined the GE Oil & Gas business as Chief Communications Officer in 2013 and embarked on a series of experiments with a cohort of twenty to forty high potential leaders whom the company had determined could be even bigger leaders. These employees had diverse professional backgrounds, e.g. engineering, sales, commercial, finance, and supply chain. Becky and the team then asked, 'What would it be like to take this cohort and super charge it digitally?'

The communications team then developed a specific training programme for this cohort and focused it on how they might use their influence. As Becky put it: 'You are a knowledgeable professional, so how do you translate your knowledge and experience into dialogue and conversation in social domains?'

As part of the training, Becky and her team prepared the cohort to showcase their digital know-how at the GE Oil & Gas Annual Meeting, normally held in January/February of every year. This involved providing them with information on what the agenda would be at the annual meeting and what new technology would be unveiled. Using social channels such as Twitter, these digital ambassadors got the opportunity to bring to light socially what they had learned in the training programme, and they were able to provide a window for those not present at the annual meeting to experience socially what had gone on at the meeting.

Other aspects of training included a basic briefing on the

different platforms, e.g. Twitter, LinkedIn and Facebook. The easiest to execute for business, it was decided, were LinkedIn and Twitter. Becky's team covered how content is created and disseminated on these platforms. The team co-created content with the cohort. Some members of the cohort retweeted GE content; some were inspired by GE content to create their own.

Analysis Reveals Gaps And Choices

Becky explained that there were two things she wanted to show through the experiment:

GE Oil & Gas employees are experts in their field and have something to share that has value to the outside audience. If that value ends up translating into a commercial transaction, or at the very least generates goodwill and positive mindshare about what's happening at GE Oil & Gas, that's a win.

Secondly, the digital conversation could result into commercial transactions, and for that reason, Becky says they decided to focus time and effort mainly on LinkedIn, where the experiment revealed there are a lot more people doing business. On LinkedIn, people tend to have one or more of the following goals:

- Seeking knowledge on how to use their equipment

- Trying to solve problems in their day to day lives

- Wanting to find out what is new in the industry

Also, the technology of LinkedIn made it easy to connect to a transaction platform on the company side – like a highway.

Setting guidelines isn't enough. As a result of the experiment, Becky says the team realised they needed to give people permission visibly and deliberately. Contrary to the idea that only the most senior person in the team can have a voice, Becky says, 'We needed to say to employees: it's OK to have a voice. Own what you know and share it.'

Employees who were unsure of participating were offered training to help them get engaged. Becky reflects on the experiment with the cohort and notes, 'We realised that if we want employees to use their networks, we need to communicate to them in that way.'

Instead of producing the usual long newsletters and white papers with detailed stories and news, the communication team provide 'socially digestible' terms for employees to share. This is called a 'monthly brew' at GE

Oil & Gas, and has content in hashtag form for easy sharing on social media.

FIGURE 3: MONTHLY BREW SHARED AT GE OIL & GAS, AUGUST 2015 EDITION

August Brew - GE Oil & Gas Content

The Power of One
#ageofgas | #gas | #power | @ge_oilandgas

1% can make a big difference. Wondering just how big? Ashley Haynes-Gaspar, Software & Services, General Manager, GE Oil & Gas offers insight into the power of the Industrial Internet and what GE calls The Power of One – the idea that GE can help its customers to harness the vast new sources of data that the Industrial Internet opens up in order to make their operations more efficient and productive. Click here to learn more.

Sample Tweets

- The power of 1% can make a big difference in #oilandgas. Take a look at how the #industrialinternet can unlock valuable insights invent.ge/1h28m7m.
- What happens when 50 billion machines become connected? invent.ge/1h28m7m.

These smart pigs are well-travelled
#pipeline | #smarttechnology | @ge_oilandgas

PII's 'smart pigs' have a good track record when it comes to how many regions they've been through and how many defects they've correctly identified (over 110MII). Take a look at the different pipeline technologies that have been used to inspect over 1.1km of pipeline worldwide.

Sample Tweets

- These smart pigs are well-travelled, inspecting over 1.1M km of pipeline worldwide via @ge_oilandgas invent.ge/1K1Gebk.
- These smart pigs have gathered data from over 1.1M km of pipeline. Take a look at which regions they've travelled. invent.ge/1K1Gebk

#OE15 is just around the corner
#OE15 | @SPE_OE | @ge_oilandgas

SPE Offshore Europe is just around the corner. Support our team in #Aberdeen as they tackle issues head on through a series of #techtalks and demos (find the list here). Our leaders will be in the spotlight sharing best practices, career advice and tech developments. Keep an eye out for sharable content throughout the upcoming weeks.

Sample Tweets

- How can @ge_oilandgas help #fuelthefuture of the offshore industry? Find out at our #OE15 #techtalks https://www.geoilandgas.com/oe
- At #OE15? Stop by booth 5B70 to meet @ge_oilandgas experts and discover how we can partner with you https://www.geoilandgas.com/oe

#FF #FOLLOWFRIDAY

This Friday, challenge yourself to follow two new influencers on LinkedIn or Twitter to keep up with industry trends. Take a look at these key influencers:

 James Herron
European Oil Editor, Bloomberg, London

 Will Kennedy
Managing editor for energy and commodities at Bloomberg News in London

TWEETABLE TIP ✅

You have 140 characters to express yourself. Add in a link and you're down to 118. An image? You're down another 23 characters. Knowing shortened Twitter lingo is an important part of crafting your tweet (and still making sense). It's easy to fall behind with Twitter abbreviations and acronyms, so here are a few to get you started:

RT = Retweet
MT = Modified Tweet. (Use this when you copy and paste someone's tweet but add your own comment, because you had to shorten the original tweet to make everything fit.)
ICYMI = In case you missed it
TBH = To be honest
TTQRT = Thanks for the RT
IMO = In my opinion
HT = Hat tip. Use this to give a nod to someone who shared the original content (similar to via)

To learn more Twitter lingo, click here.

Becky notes that GE Oil & Gas needed to be more diligent about linking people to the sales pipeline. Keys areas to focus on were letting people buy stuff and helping them learn about stuff they've already bought. There are currently experiments delving into these areas.

Social As An Enabler

What would be a good outcome for GE Oil & Gas? Becky explains that social is an enabler that allows GE Oil & Gas:

- To do more commercial transactions that stem from digital interactions

- To generate goodwill and positive mindshare so that people looking for information find positive information

- To position GE Oil & Gas employees as thought leaders in their field so that they draw potential and existing customers into a deeper conversation that might lead to more business relationships.

Becky explains that in the past, technical experts, for instance, would get an outlet mainly through conferences, where the conversation would be one to many people sitting inside a room somewhere. She says, 'Thanks to digital platforms, more people can now fit inside that room.'

Social media participation gives power to conversations, multiplying the 'many people' exponentially.

Oil & Gas: A Shy Industry

Social media took off in the B2C space and has been coming along in B2B. Some industries, such as oil and gas, have not come along as quickly as others. The oil and gas industry is known for being risk adverse, and not being as quick to take on new technology until it's tried and tested or an industrial disaster signals a clear need for change.

In discussing the progress of social media in oil and gas, Becky explains that the industry is not particularly outspoken, but cites GE Oil & Gas's recent collaboration with Statoil and how social played a role in it. There are websites and Twitter handles attributed to 'Powering Collaboration' which is a joint initiative between Statoil and GE Oil & Gas. Statoil is perceived as being progressive and a visionary in the oil and gas industry, and, perhaps as a result of its inherent culture, it provides a conducive environment for such collaboration.

What GE Measures

GE Oil & Gas measures likes and shares internally, followers and likes externally. In fact, the business unit recently crossed the 100,000 followers mark[22] on LinkedIn, a milestone achieved through organic social media activity. Becky and her team capture progress on other externally-facing social channels. For instance, GE Oil & Gas added over 3,000 followers on Twitter in the second quarter of 2015. Share of voice (SoV) is also measured by mention, as shown in the pie chart for the same quarter in 2015.

FIGURE 4: SHARE OF VOICE, SECOND QUARTER 2015 BRAND INSIGHTS REPORT AT GE OIL & GAS

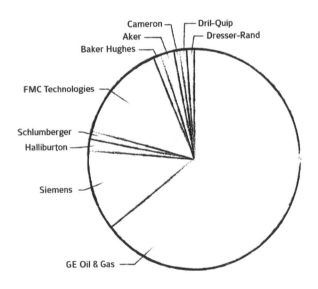

---

22 This was measured as at end August 2015

Here are customer and employee focussed stats based on GE Oil & Gas's second quarter (Q2) 2015 performance:

TABLE 4: CUSTOMER FOCUSSED STATS, SECOND QUARTER 2015 AT GE OIL & GAS

Metrics	Q2 2015
Leads generated	1,910
Leads turned to opportunities	12

Becky explains that part of measuring progress internally is ensuring employee engagement. Lorenzo Simonelli, CEO of GE Oil & Gas, writes on an internal blog. Engagement on that blog is captured below:

TABLE 5: EMPLOYEE FOCUSSED STATS, SECOND QUARTER 2015 AT GE OIL & GAS

Metrics	Q2 2015
New subscribers to Lorenzo Simonelli's internal blog	172
New posts on Lorenzo's blog, including posts from guest bloggers elected by Lorenzo	10

A recent employee channel preference audit with 1,670 respondents revealed that employees preferred to receive company news from their manager through all-employee meetings or calls and email. It also revealed that employees checked company news online in the mornings, on Mondays and Fridays. Employees wanted news to be more tailored and relevant to their role and/or interests as well as accessible via mobile phones.

Becky has personally had a whirlwind of engagement from the oil and gas community due to her online activity. Considering that Becky only arrived in the oil and gas industry two years ago, she says that up to a third of her LinkedIn connections are from oil and gas. A lot of the conversation for Becky has been about diversity in the industry for women and minority groups. Becky couldn't be more pleased with the attraction and engagement she gets on this subject.

About Becky @ GE Oil & Gas

After working with companies such as Wall Street Journal and Rudy Finn and with over fifteen years' experience in journalism and communication, Becky joined GE in 2010 as Global Employee Communications Leader based in London, UK. Becky had significant involvement with developing new social tools and contemporising the commercial process. Today, Becky is engaging and motivating employees to be GE brand ambassadors and has become an ambassador herself, not just on digital platforms, but as a strong, inspiring voice for diversity on behalf of women and minority groups in the oil and gas industry.

At the end of Step Two, reflect on:

- Do you have a clearly formulated strategy for your social media programmes?

- Have you conducted an employee and/or audience segmentation exercise?

- Do you understand the gap between where your organisation is and what where you'd like it to be?

- Have you identified early adopters who are passionate about social media and can act as ambassadors throughout the business?

- Have you considered training content and tool kits to make it easier for employees to participate?

- How will you measure the 'right' things, such as number of articles or videos published, proportion of employees trained and overall employee scale of influence?

PART 4 – STEP 3: MOVE INTO ACTION!

The tiniest of actions is always better than the boldest of intentions

Robin Sharma

Part 4 highlights:

- Action learning could be used to promote a virtuous cycle of learning and changing

- Key elements for implementing the virtuous cycle are: feedback, empowerment and boundaries, training and support, and rewards and recognition

- Lead the change and then shift roles to a consulting or collaborative style

- Embed the culture long term through training, support and role modelling the new behaviours

- Sustain momentum through clear links to business goals and relevant proof of success.

13. THE VIRTUOUS CYCLE OF LEARNING AND CHANGING

Early applications of organisation development were guided by work on action technologies with learning-based approaches such as action learning (Cummings, 2004). Originating with Reginald Revan's work in 1983, researchers such as Dixon (1998) believe that this kind of learning has the potential to change both organisations and participants as it moves beyond a problem-solving focus of action research and treats change as a continuous learning and transformation process (Greenwood, Foote, & Harkavy, 1993; Cummings, 2004).

While sustainable change should be continuous, with small but frequent improvements, organisations in fast-paced environments face significant pressure to move quickly (Vaill, 1989, as cited in Cummings, 2004). Action learning provides the mechanism to reflect on actions and underlying assumptions so that it becomes the bridge between learning and transformational change (Limerick, Passfield, & Cunnington, 1994). It involves interrelated actions that comprise an iterative learning process. As employees move through these activities they learn how to change and improve the organisation, their own work behaviours and interactions (Cummings, 2004). This is the virtuous cycle of learning and changing.

FIGURE 5: ACTION LEARNING – LEARNING AND CHANGING

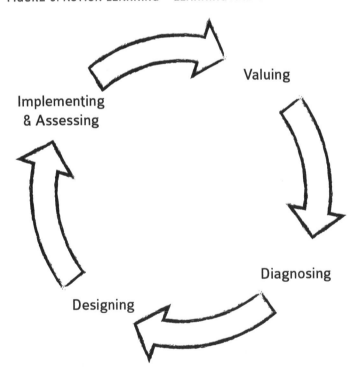

With a clear, widely-understood vision in hand, action learning could enable organisations to clarify the values that will guide the change process explicitly. This could mean realigning certain values present in the status quo as discussed in a previous section. What emerges is an iterative process important for propelling learning and change during social media programmes.

Let's discuss the essence of the action learning cycle.

The outcome of 'valuing' is usually a vision statement that explains the values guiding the change (Cummings, 2004). This vision may be reassessed and modified as progress is made through the cycle of learning activities (Greenwood, Foote, & Harkavy, 1993) but it needs to be established early on in affirming your employees (see Part 2).

'Diagnosing' the organisation involves revealing the gaps. It means asking questions such as: 'What needs to change?' As a manager, it means you putting a mirror up in front of the organisation and showing the space between the desired values (for employee participation to be an established behaviour) and the status quo (how employees are behaving at the moment). It allows continual assessment and improvement in the organisation in a valued direction (Cummings, 2004). This stage could unveil additional complexities if the current corporate culture is significantly at odds with the desired state of things. The job of a social media manager might be harder, but not impossible if there is senior management support.

The 'designing' stage is usually flexible and iterative to allow participants to modify changes as they learn how to enact them behaviourally (Cummings, 2004; Greenwood *et al*, 2003). Going through this stage will raise questions about the current state and end state of the organisation while piecing together a detailed plan to close the gaps revealed in the diagnosing stage. While designing a plan for action, experiments and pilot projects may happen in small pockets of the organisation. This is the time to leverage your small but influential community of social media early adopters – you need your ambassadors as part of your strategic planning. At the end of the designing stage, you should not only have a plan but have a reasonable idea of what could work and what will not. You'll know this because you have tested out some ideas in a small, controlled way. The outcome has now influenced how the design for action turns out.

The 'Implementing & Assessing' is associated with actually 'doing' the change. During the interviews I carried out, the following elements emerged as crucial for the interlinked process of Implementing-Assessing-Implementing:

- Feedback

- Empowerment with boundaries

- Training & Support

- Rewards & Recognition.

I will take each of these in turn and highlight what you should be looking out for as a social media manager or leader in the organisation.

Feedback

When a plan is in motion, whether through pilot projects or controlled experiments, feedback should be solicited from employees where possible. This may be done through internal surveys, blog commentary and face-to-face interviews. Aside from pilot projects and experiments, those I interviewed collected feedback about employee. Such feedback came formally and informally through open dialogue and in online communities. The frequency, sincerity and method of feedback tended to depend partially on corporate culture. For instance, feedback was more readily available if there was normally a culture of feedback in the organisation.

Some social media managers told me that feedback from customers and suppliers was also collected doing pilot projects to determine if the brand messages were getting through.

One external consultant noted, 'There was a team of people interacting with our customers all day, every day, so we were continuously getting feedback.'

The above comment reveals that feedback is also offline, not just virtual (online).

Most importantly, it was clear from some of my discussions that feedback had enabled organisations to increase participation significantly as they took it on board, using it to tweak training and to make communication better tailored to the different employee groups.

Empowerment With Boundaries

For employees to participate effectively, they need to be empowered, which means removing barriers so that the organisational environment supports changed behaviours and new ways of thinking. Empowerment could unfreeze the organisation to allow mobilisation for unlearning past behaviour (O'Keeffe, 2002; McHugh, Groves, & Alker, 1998; Wang & Ahmed, 2003). Barriers to empowerment include ill-aligned systems, management style, lack of information and lack of training (Kotter & Cohen, 2002). Therefore, structures, systems and processes must support new behaviours (Kotter & Cohen, 2002; Balogun & Hope-Hailey, 2004) otherwise employees will soon fall out of the new [participation] behaviour.

Some organisations operate within strict boundaries. Such firms appear to prefer pre-defined roles and responsibility, and put great emphasis on formal hierarchy (Bradley & McDonald, 2011). Researchers argue that these organisations will struggle to imbibe a social culture, and there was some evidence to support this in my research with social media managers.

Conversely, some researchers, such as Scott-Ladd & Chan (2004), believe clear boundaries are crucial for effective participation. While this appears to conflict with the notion of employee engagement, Brown & Eisenhardt (1997) in their paper 'The Art of Continuous Change: Linking Complexity Theory and Time-paced Evolution in Relentlessly Shifting Organizations' describe the need for balance when they argue, 'Too little structure makes it hard to coordinate change. Too much structure makes it hard to move.'

It makes sense that the risk of a crisis situation erupting in an organisation increases as more employees participate. How can a manager achieve the balance that Brown & Eisenhardt write about? Some practitioners noted that they achieved some balance between empowerment and boundaries by enacting a policy with clear guidelines about what employees can do on social media. As well as encouraging the use of social media, they set boundaries at the same time. I will discuss training and support shortly, but part of achieving balance will be through educational and training programmes designed to provide the knowledge and tools for using social media appropriately within an organisation. In addition, support from senior and middle management and training often give employees the confidence they need to overcome fears associated with social media use, as well as flexibility within their role to try new things. One manager summarised how the delicate balance between empowerment and boundaries was propelled in one organisation:

'Flexibility exists in a person's role to take on additional projects. The environment encourages experimentation and personal knowledge acquisition.'

Real changes in behaviour happened after providing practical training that required attendees to start, for example, their own Twitter account and update it regularly with posts and pictures. One social business leader concluded: 'It was learning by doing'.

Training And Support

As a minimum, all employees will need basic training on social media policies and guidelines, regardless of role or interest. This is the standard in large social media active organisations. It will take time, and it will likely need to be a phased process with targets to train certain levels of employees [using employee segmentation data] first, then move to a different group of staff and so on until the majority of employees are trained. Set a target, e.g. 75% of employees in a twelve-month period. The level and content of the training will vary between participants based on employee segmentation needs and the portion of an employee's role that requires social media. Some will need very basic training consisting of a code of conduct and guidelines, while others requiring more advanced tiered training.

When it comes to training, employees can have as much of it as you can give, but if they don't believe in it – that is, if they don't make a personal connection to the vision of the business being translated in part by social media programmes – they won't use it. Therefore, participation is voluntary with social media managers often starting with early adopters who already have a passion for social media.

Rewards And Recognition

During my research, some managers I spoke with used recognition more than rewards in motivating employees. Recognition programmes include peer-recommendations by rating systems and recognition badges that employees could show off on their internal online profiles. The area of rewards and recognition appeared to be a work-in-progress in many organisations. There are varying approaches and reward systems used across global organisations. One consultant commented that the area of rewards and recognition is one of the key elements that require community feedback in order to improve current practices.

Susan Emerick notes in my interview with her, 'Early adopters are helping us through feedback to shape our reward and recognition programmes and are helping us understand what would be of value to them.'

Social media change requires sustained commitment over time in order to become an authority figure – to become influential. In the end, people are different, so it might not be that interesting for some even with training and support.

In motivating people to take part in social programmes, one external consultant noted that monetary rewards had no impact at all, so they were dropped for other recognition programmes.

Aside from the elements discussed here, cross-functional teams and communities play a significant role in fostering change and propelling the virtuous cycle. Building lasting communities is core to implementing the change required for employee participation in social programmes, particularly the need to break down silos within the organisations.

Few managers discussed the Hub & Spoke Model. This model consists of a cross-functional team consisting of multiple stakeholders across the organisation, e.g. HR, marketing and operations (the 'Hub'), that sits at the centre of the organisation to guide and provide resources to the 'Spoke'. This could be local teams implementing the social media change in their business unit or geographical region. This model works in organisations such as IBM and EMC[2].

Here's an excerpt from a recent article in *AdWeek* magazine on how IBM got mass employee participation (Heine, 2015):

How IBM got 1,000 Staffers to become brand advocates on social media

---

IBM has had a pretty tech-savvy workforce since it was founded in 1911. It is Big Blue we are talking about here, after all.

But it wasn't until a year ago that the Armonk, N.Y.-based Company started working with Dynamic Signal to see what would happen if its sales force and other marketing employees promoted its software products using their personal social-media accounts. IBM created an internal online hub that allowed employees to share promotions easily on Twitter, LinkedIn and Facebook, while they could also privately pass information back and forth to help their marketing and sales.

A thousand employees have participated in the program, which gives them about six pieces of content every day they can choose to share or not share with their followers.

'It's not a requirement at all, but it's something that, if they do it, they get recognized for it,' Amber Armstrong, program director at IBM Marketing Digital, told *Adweek*.

'And the program has been a resounding success with more IBM employees "banging down the door" to participate,' she said.

Here is one of the reasons why: the company late last year launched a business-to-business appeal called #NewWayToWork, which accrued 120 million digital impressions and drove 141,000 clicks to campaign content, thanks largely to the employees sharing content through Dynamic Signal's VoiceStorm software. Interestingly, IBM staffers are only incentivized by a points-based leader board—they're not getting bonuses, though Armstrong said that it's clearly helping members make sales.

14. LEAD IT, THEN LEAVE IT

In discussing the end of a change process, Kanter (2005) notes, 'Don't launch and leave'. There are several elements to build before a change is truly on the way. Through my research, I discovered that social media change leaders didn't 'launch and leave'. However, there are shifts in roles where a leader could go from leading a change to supporting from the sidelines. Therefore in one sense, they do launch and then leave, but it is more like leading it to a point and then leaving that leadership position to act as a supportive advisor or consultant.

The ideal situation is that the social media manager does such a great job of leading the change that the rest runs itself. You basically work yourself out of a job, or go to another business unit and instigate the same changes, or act as an advisor where your role takes a different form. It's good when this happens because it means you have succeeded.

Before leaving the position of leadership for social media change, a social media manager needs to ensure a few elements are present in the business:

- Embedded new culture

- Continued support for empowerment

- Sustained momentum.

Let's discuss these in turn so that you get the gist.

Embedding A New Culture

Wenger, McDermott & Synder (2002) write that sustaining the momentum of participation in communities requires the establishment of the new culture. 'Sustaining' implies a continuous learning process that is self-sustaining, and it should grow (Bradley & McDonald, 2011). To achieve this, social media managers will need to help their organisation focus on embedding the new culture through executive commitment and securing continuity for the changes – essentially, refreezing the organisation (Kurt Lewin's change model in Part 3).

Kotter & Cohen (2002) advise, 'Keep a change in place by helping to create a new, supportive and sufficiently strong organisational culture.' The authors go further to suggest using the power of culture to help make transformation[23] stick, ensuring the vision is linked to everything the division does. Culture is relevant throughout the change process. Moreover, learning seems intertwined with culture at every stage, prompting some researchers like Gherardi & Nicolini (2001) to suggest that learning is intrinsic to the practices that sustain an organisation. Furthermore, a learning culture may be promoted through renewal workshops, and by developing new leadership.

Change is only likely if someone is [explicitly] responsible for leading that change (Balogun & Hope-Hailey, 2004). That someone may well be you, the marketing or business manager, a social media or community manager or a team of people working equally to lead the change. With that in mind, consideration needs to be given to change roles, i.e. whether the change will be managed by a change team, an internal leader or external consultant. The change leader or team should be cognisant of continuity in leadership and provide training and mentoring for new members and leaders-to-be.

A brief comment about your leadership style as you lead the change:

---

23   Interesting June 2015 article on transformational change here https://www.linkedin.com/pulse/changing-organizational-culture-world-rob-peters?trk=hp-feed-article-title

TIP

Depending on the initial state of the organisation, you may move from a directive style to a more consultative or collaborative style (Dunphy & Stace, 1993) *as you shift from leading to supporting or advising it.*

Continued Support For Empowerment

The role of empowerment in changing is critical because it enables employees to act out the 'right' behaviours. It enables employees to participate in social media programmes. Empowered people change a culture, and strong cultures support the empowerment process by providing continuity, clarity and consistency (Mallak & Kurstedt, 1996).

New members in a team or organisation may move from acknowledging new cultures to empowerment and then intervening with other team members when there are diversions from the new norms. As time progresses, new members may be found providing feedback in cases of inconsistencies in culture or behaviour.

Hendry's analogy in his 1996 paper provides some clarity:

Children do not start out with values. They absorb them unwittingly from their parents and (especially) from interaction with their peers. In the process, they test out for themselves what values work in the environments in which they have to survive.

These changes in new members could perhaps happen by observation of the culture, or through a series of training sessions (Kotter & Cohen, 2002).

Sustained Momentum

'There's no point you get to and think: that's it. I'm done!' This comment from a social media manager resonated with all those I interviewed. Many expressed the need to continue igniting participation, using feedback to improve and add to best practices. They also echoed the need for measurement as 'physical proof' to sustain the change so that it is not just a fad. Linking social media change to business objectives and showing employees the value they add by participating are essential to sustaining momentum, as this comment by an external consultant reveals:

'We used a managed approach – measuring progress towards the business objectives. People could see why the community was there, their role in it and the value it added to their business units.'

Some of those who I interviewed did not undergo a shift in role *per se* because they had moved around the organisation, starting implementations and moving on to the next location or business unit to lead a similar change. However, a few described their initial role as one of an evangelist, role modelling the change by using social media themselves to spread interest. As the change progressed, their role became one of a consultant, available if teams or individuals needed guidance. One manager moved from leading technical training to being a consultant. His hands were off once the teams were well on the way to implementation. As a social media manager, you have to scale and give other people empowerment for execution.

To conclude the three-step framework, I realise that in the past few years some organisations have become very good at employee advocacy through social media programmes. But recent discussions suggest that many business-to-business operations are still experimenting and researching social media to make it relevant and effective in their businesses. Few organisations have not embarked on using social media as a tool for business impact, but some organisations leave social media involvement to the marketing team, hence limiting participation and opportunities to spread thought leadership across the organisation.

It may be a few years before social media becomes linked to everything that organisations do – even for organisations mature in social media. Evidence in my research of time spent identifying gaps to close in the organisation, designing social media change and implementing the plans paints a picture of a continuous iterative process that could eventually lead to embedding a social media culture that changes organisation-wide behaviour. Meaningful measurement metrics that subsequently show positive impact on the business are likely to fuel the affirmation that employees need to change, creating a truly virtuous cycle.

15. INSIGHT: SAS SOFTWARE

Interview With Alli Soule, Social Media Employee Engagement And Education Specialist At SAS

Date of Interview: 30 July 2015

About SAS

SAS was founded in 1976 by a university professor, James Goodnight, while he was at North Carolina State University in the US. SAS now has over 13,000 employees and offices internationally, including in Glasgow and London in the UK.

SAS is a business analytics software company that works with companies across multiple industries such as oil and gas, banking, and healthcare. They create and market software that helps businesses make decisions based on the data that companies accumulate. This includes structured and unstructured data. As SAS is a business-to-business company, its software is made to scale so that it can take billions of rows of data and do sophisticated analysis. Therefore, SAS is very much a scientific company with mainly technical knowledge workers.

The SAS Culture

SAS is arguably more well-known for its company culture than its products. It ranks in the Top 5 every year, including in the Fortune 100 Best Companies to Work 2015 list[24] where SAS ranks No. 4.

Alli explains that this list has an extensive criteria, including the benefits and inherent philosophy that companies might have, employee engagement, and so on. Alli believes that SAS's culture has played a huge role in the use of social media at work. Employees have several benefits, such as a gym, café and healthcare centre on the SAS campus. These may appear to be cushy perks, but Alli explains that they show SAS encourages work-life balance and thus produces happier employees.

She notes, 'SAS management trusts its employees and believes that they won't abuse the privileges they have.

---

24 Check out http://www.greatplacetowork.com/best-companies/100-best-companies-to-work-for#sthash.qn6Q4AGx.dpbs for the Fortune 100 list, accessed 24 September 2015

This has trickled into social media participation. SAS trusts employees to do the right thing.'

When social media took off at SAS, the company made an organised push, and even hired a social media manager in 2008 to secure a clear point of contact.

An Organised Push

SAS began to identify key responsibilities within the social media initiative, determining who was accountable for what. It developed relevant guidelines that were based on the fundamental trust SAS had for its employees.

Alli says, 'SAS basically said to its employees: "We trust you to represent us professionally face-to-face and on the phone, so we also trust you to represent us on social media in a professional manner".'

Alli explains that SAS's core values are supported by its social media activities. They are:

- Be approachable

- Be customer-driven

- Be swift and agile

- Be innovative

- Be trustworthy and transparent.

Social media plays into all SAS's core values and sits beautifully with its business goals and brand image. Alli says, 'For instance, social media is innovative, and to be successful, a company needs to be swift and agile as well as customer-driven.'

In addition, social media is all about being transparent. Becoming a social business was therefore a natural transformation.

Leadership supported the social media push verbally and also invested in hiring social media roles. This allowed a push into action early on, culminating in the creation of a Global Social Media Manager job in 2008.

'Leadership sees so much value in this that they are going to pay people to do it as a full time job.'

That position now has five direct reports, and Alli is one of them.

Supportive Leaders Participate

SAS has an internal social media network called 'The Hub', built on the SocialCast platform. It is a kind of Facebook for SAS employees. Periodically, SAS leadership engages on this platform to listen to what employees are saying and respond to things, such as the time a rumour started about SAS (a privately held company) being sold. The CEO used The Hub to dispel the rumours.

Alli laughs as she narrates the joke her CEO made: 'He posted: *We are not being sold. And if anyone is selling the company without my knowledge, please stop!*'

Alli estimates that at least 30% of the core executives at SAS blog regularly, both internally and externally, including the Chief Marketing Officer and Head of Sales. SAS even has a blog, The Corner Office[25], which features posts authored solely by executives. Many leaders have Twitter accounts as it's a developing channel for SAS.

What Alli describes is great, and perhaps unprecedented. Many companies I interviewed and surveyed have noted some degree of lacking in executive participation. The experience at SAS appears to stem from an inherent supportive culture.

Communicating Through All Channels

One of the reasons Alli was brought in (aside from the fact that she's amazing!) was because she has a mass

---

25   Check out The Corner Office at http://blogs.sas.com/content/corneroffice/

communication and internal communication back-ground. Internal communication, she believes, is the crux of getting any employee advocacy programme off the ground. The success of such programmes depends on continuously communicating the vision, and also showcasing employees who are already doing this. Alli believes this builds on the value of social media in the company.

SAS has a company Intranet managed by the internal communications team. The team publishes five to seven news stories daily, ensuring that the news is not stale, and also publish well-put-together videos for employees. Articles are meant for a general employee audience, and topics range from company events and initiatives to customer stories to employee spotlights. Other commu-nication channels used in SAS are:

- The Hub, an internal social network platform with special interest groups much like Facebook

- The Sales Update, a daily email newsletter pub-lishing articles targeting SAS's sales and marketing departments

- Internal blogs communicating information on varied subjects, including social media. Alli's team blog, the Social Soup, posts regularly on topics such as emerging digital technology, abbreviated social media lessons via the #TipOfTheWeek series and entertaining posts linking to random holidays, e.g. National Scotch Day (usually in July), and other trending topics. Alli says, 'Some of these seeming ridiculous but humorous posts often draw people back to your social profile and generate new followers.'

Alli and the team use these platforms to communicate available training and blogging tips to the wider employee community.

Tell It To Them Simply

Developing SAS's social media guidelines has been a major collaboration between its legal and HR teams. There's an entire section in the HR policy devoted specifically to social media use. Alli explains that once the teams knew what to include in the guidelines, they spent a lot of time refining them to ensure they were simple and readable.

From in-house training materials, their blog and general information about SAS's participation on social, the Corporate Social Media Team maintains a site accessible from SAS's Intranet called the 'Social Media Resource Portal'. The Portal also contains SAS's social media policies and guidelines.

The team wanted to give employees options when it came to social media guidelines: they knew some employees just wanted to skim through a document so they could quickly understand the basic philosophy of social media use at SAS. Other employees wanted more granular explanations and examples. To that end, there are two variations of SAS's social media policies:

1. Employee Social Media Fundamentals: five simplified points summarising SAS's policies for employee social media use.

2. Employee Social Media Guidelines: a more extensive explanation of subjects like SAS's Approach to Social Media; employee participation; and Confidentiality, Customer and User Conversations.

Additionally, some social networks present the need for platform-specific employee guidelines. Those guidelines can be found on corresponding pages of the Social Media Resource Portal under a menu called Channels 101, as shown in the screenshot below, which offers a breakdown of every social media channel where SAS has a presence.

FIGURE 7: SAS SOCIAL MEDIA RESOURCE PORTAL

For instance, there are guidelines for individual LinkedIn accounts or those wanting to set up LinkedIn groups. The same guidance exists for Twitter. Channels 101 also provides searchable directories where employees can find secondary SAS accounts relating to different products and industries.

Significant effort has been dedicated to providing clear, simple guidelines to employees. These are based on the results of an employee survey conducted at SAS where employees were asked questions like: 'What prevents you from using social media?'

SAS got plenty of feedback from employees on the kind of training they believed was needed, and what stopped them from getting involved in social media for their jobs. Some of the feedback was around guidelines and policies.

Alli says, 'A lot of employees were worried they were going to say the wrong things and get into trouble.'

With the Portal, employees with questions know where to find answers. If they don't find what they are looking for, they can contact a member of the social media team.

What SAS Measures

Alli admits that measuring social media effort is constantly evolving. At present, the team puts out an annual report on social activity covering elements such as:

- Social engagement (mentions, likes, comments, shares, etc.) by channel

- Number of posts by channel and estimated click-through rates

- Top-performing content and content types (e.g. photos versus links versus graphics, etc.)

• Overall growth of SAS accounts online

• Page hits and actions taken on sas.com initiated by a social media post.

Aside from these measures, SAS also has a robust social listening[26] programme where elements of SAS's online presence is monitored during specific periods of time, e.g. during events. Social listening enables SAS to monitor the buzz and sentiment generated by its brand online. SAS is focussed on engagement: 'Is anyone retweeting our tweet, commenting on our LinkedIn posts or engaging with us in any way?'

Therefore, social engagement numbers are very important to SAS as they reveal a lot about the impact of its social media efforts.

Here are some stats showing the percentage increase in traffic from 2014 to 2015 to SAS's main website, sas.com:

---

26 Social listening is the art of monitoring the sentiment and reaction around a brand on social media sites such as Twitter. This information can be used to devise improved strategies of how to engage with customers on and offline.

TABLE 6: SAS SOCIAL MEDIA STATS 2014/15

Social Media Channel	% traffic increase from 2014 to 2015
LinkedIn	81
Twitter	86
Facebook	14
Blogger	2
Stack Overflow	42

These stats come from its social media channels; that is, social media is driving people to sas.com, where SAS hope they are taking some sort of action like registering for events, downloading white papers or just learning about products and services.

A Supporting Role For Action

In Alli's global role, she provides one-on-one consultations to individuals having challenges on social media as they use it. She also consults with managers who want their team to be active online, for instance on Twitter, but are not sure how other teams are using it and whether it makes sense to use it.

Alli says, 'I meet with the team, discuss the tools with them and basically act in a sort of consultancy role. If the tool is right for them, I develop and deliver a training curriculum specifically for the team.'

Alli is also involved in developing training certification programmes at SAS for social media. These are e-learning courses intended for any employee who wishes to become better acclimatised to using social media in his or her job.

The certification programme hopes to fulfil a number of purposes by:

- Providing training for an additional communications outlet for SAS employee subject-matter experts to share their knowledge

- Giving employees a way to build their personal brands or become social influencers

- Administering general how-to training so employees can use social media to do their jobs more efficiently.

Alli notes that this is empowering for employees. It reflects positively on the employee, and indirectly on the SAS brand as these people are willing to talk about what they are doing on social media.

Alli and the team are working very closely with Internal

Communications and HR in this effort because of the overlap with other employee programmes, e.g. the suggestion that gaining social media certification could potentially become a factor in promotions and pay rises. Maintaining open collaboration with Internal Communications and HR allows the Corporate Social Media Team to help repurpose programmes for other uses across the company.

How Alli Keeps It Together

Social media remains optional at SAS so it's not something being crammed down everybody's throat. Alli sees this as a good thing because she can approach things fairly casually and say, 'Hey, if you're interested, these resources are available!'

Indeed, social media is not for everyone, but Alli supports people who want to participate. She and her team provide guidance to those new to the organisation and are easing into the culture. Using the existing communication channels, she spends time correcting and clarifying misconceptions around the use of social media, which can be challenging for her as she doesn't want to discourage employees or appear to be policing them. Her team uses a delicate balance of praise and correction to keep social media participation on track and within the guidelines.

To motivate employees, the team uses the available communication channels to give 'shout-outs' to those doing it right as a way of recognition. Looking ahead, the team hopes to reward socially active employees with access to paid social media tools as well as recognising a 'Social Media Employee of the Month'.

Finally, Alli offers guidance for posting SAS content versus non-SAS content. She refers to the 4-1-1 rule:

- Post four pieces of non-SAS content

- Post one piece of content created by SAS or the employee

- Post one piece that is fun and entertaining.

This is a fluid rule at SAS, but it gives employees an idea of what will give them the most online engagement. This sits well with recent research showing that allowing only work-related content could adversely affect an employee's participation in social media at work, and even reduce the internal readership of blog posts (Huang, Singh, & Ghose, 2015). Hence, the fluid rule at SAS appears reasonable and set to keep employees motivated and participating.

About Alli @SAS

Alli Soule joined SAS as a Senior Communications Specialist in 2010. Being a natural communicator, she continues to be a force behind sustaining employee participation and engagement at SAS. Since attending a summer programme at the University of Stirling, Alli has become an enduring admirer of Scotland. She can be contacted on Twitter **@allisoule**

At the end of Step Three, reflect on:

- How will you create a virtuous learning cycle that fosters the required change? Could the principles of action learning help you achieve this?

- Do you have a process for collecting and considering employee feedback? How have you leveraged early adopters in strategic planning and iteration of practices?

- Do you have established and communicated boundaries through policy, guidelines, training and executive support? How empowered are employees as a result of these boundaries?

- Have you planned or delivered basic training to all or a majority of your employees, with varying levels of training for employees with active involvement in social programmes?

- Do you have a way to recognise and celebrate early wins?

- Are you considering how you will step out of the way and shift into a more consulting collaborative style after you have led the change?

- How will you ensure the new culture is embedded in your organisation?

- How will you support empowerment and sustain momentum?

- Have you developed a set of metrics that links to business goals in order to provide physical proof of achievements?

SUMMARY AND DOWNLOADS

In summary, there are six main recommendations for driving employee participation that you should take away from this book. They are:

1. Invest in frequent experimentation and aim to formalise processes and provide meaningful measurements over the longer term.

2. Use cross-functional teams and allow personal development and contribution.

3. Promote a shared vision and share responsibility between employees and the organisation to create commitment to social media change.

4. Include employees and their feedback in strategic planning and reviewing guidelines.

5. Support employees by providing resources for identifying and resolving cultural misalignment, provide training and act out values

6. Empower early adopters to instigate the change, reward through recognition and showcase early achievements.

TIP

To monitor social media participation in your organisation, administer my social media participation survey to measure progress. I developed the survey in 2012 and administered it to thirty-nine social media professionals. The survey allows you to measure all three steps of the framework discussed in this book. You will be able to identify what aspects need more work and where you are doing well.

Go to www.socialmediaparticipation.com/downloads to download your free social business survey guide. The e-book guide contains a twenty-three question survey and references to other useful resources. I'd love to hear how you have used the survey so please feel free to email me at book@socialmediaparticipation.com.

PUBLICATIONS CITED

Armenakis, A., Harris, S., & Mossholder, K. (1993). Creating readiness for organizational change. *Human Relations*, 581-703.

Balogun, J., & Hope-Hailey, V. (2004). Understanding Implementation choices: The options to consider. In K. Balogun, & V. Hope-Hailey, *Exploring Strategic Change* (pp. 18-53). London: Prentice Hall/Financial Times.

Barnetta, A. (2009). *Fortune 500 companies in Second Life: Activities, their success measurement and the satisfaction level of their projects.* Zurich: Eidgenossische Technische Hochschule.

Beer, M., Eisenstat, R., & Spector, B. (1990). Why Change Programs Don't Produce Change. *Harvard Business Review*.

Bradley, A., & McDonald, M. (2011). *The Social Organization: How to use social media to tap the collective genius of your customers and employees.* Boston: Harvard Business Review Press.

Brown, S. L., & Eisenhardt, K. M. (1997). The Art of Continuous Change: Linking Complexity Theory and Time-paced Evolution in Relentlessly Shifting Organizations. *Administrative Science Quarterly*, 1-34.

Cummings, T. (2004). Organization Development and Change: Foundations and Applications. In J. Boonstra, *Dynamics of Organizational Change and Learning* (pp. 25-42). Chichester: John Wiley & Sons.

de Caluwe, L., & Vermaak, H. (2004a). Thinking about change in different colours: Multiplicity in change processes. In J. Boonstra, *Dynamics of Organizational Change and Learning* (pp. 197-226). London: John Wiley & Sons.

Dixon, N. M. (1998, March). Action Learning: More Than Just A Task Force. *Performance Improvement Quarterly*, 44-58.

Doppler, K. (2004). Managing Change Successfully: Core Questions, Issues, and Strategies. In J. Boonstra, *Dynamics of organizational learning and change* (pp. 115-32). London: John Wiley & Sons.

Dunphy, D., & Stace, D. (1993). The strategic management of corporate change. *Human Relations*.

Gherardi, S., & Nicolini, D. (2001). The sociological foundations of organizational learning. In M. Dierkes, A. Berthoin Antal, J. Child, & I. Nonaka, *Handbook of Organizational Learning & Knowledge* (pp. 35-60). Oxford: Oxford University Press.

Glew, D. J., O'Leary-Kelly, A. M., & & Van Fleet, D. D. (1995). Participation in organizations: A preview of the issues and proposed framework for future analysis. *Journal of Management*, 395-421.

Greenwood, D., Foote, W. F., & Harkavy, I. (1993). Participatory action research as a process and as a goal. *Human Relations*, 175-92.

Hebert, D. (2015, June 30). *Training Your Employees To Use Social At Work Is Only Half The Battle.* Retrieved from LinkedIn: https://www.linkedin.com/pulse/training-your-employees-use-social-work-only-half-battle-hebert?trk=hp-feed-article-title-channel-add

Heine, C. (2015, July 1). *How IBM got 1,000 staffers to become brand advocates on social media.* Retrieved from AdWeek Magazine: http://www.adweek.com/news/technology/how-ibm-got-1000-staffers-become-brand-advocates-social-media-165664?mkt_tok=3RkMMJWWfF9ws-RoluKzOZKXonjHpfsX56%2B8qX6e0lMI%2F0ER-3fOvrPUfGjI4ASsBjI%2BSLDwEYGJlv6SgFSb-bHMbJq1LgNXxE

Hendry, C. (1996). Understanding and creating organizational change through learning theory. *Human Relations*, 621-41.

Huang, Y., Singh, P. V., & Ghose, A. (2015). A Structural model of employee behavioural dynamics in enterprise social media. *Management Science*.

Kanter, R. (2005, November 17). Leadership for Change: Enduring skills for change masters. *Harvard Business School*, pp. 1-16.

Kaplan, A., & Haenlein, M. (2010). Users of the world, unite! The challenges and opportunities of social media. *Business Horizons*, 59-68.

Kotter, J., & Cohen, D. (2002). *The Heart of Change: Real Stories of How People Change their Organizations.* Boston: Harvard Business Review Press.

Lewin, K. (1946). Action research and minority problems. *Journal of social issues*, 34-46.

Limerick, D., Passfield, R., & Cunnington, B. (1994). Transformational change; Towards an action learning organization. *The learning organisation.*

Luecke, R. (2003). *Managing change and transition.* Boston: Harvard Business Press.

Mallak, L., & Kurstedt, H. (1996). Understanding and using empowerment to change organizational culture. *Industrial Management*, 8-10.

McHugh, D., Groves, D., & Alker, A. (1998). Managing learning: What do we learn from a learning organization? *The learning organization*, 209-220.

O'Keeffe, T. (2002). Organisational learning: a new perspective. *Journal of European Industrial Training*, 130-41.

Orlikowski, W. J., & Hofman, D. J. (1997). An improvisational model of change management: The case of groupware technologies. *Sloan Management Review*, 11-21.

Owyang, J., Jones, A., Tran, C., & Nguyen, A. (2011). *Social Business Readiness: How Advanced Companies Prepare Internally*. Altimeter Group.

Premo, K., & Vollmer, C. (2011, October 4). *Campaigns to capabilities: Social media and marketing 2011*. Retrieved from Strategy& (the strategy consulting group in PwC), Originally published by Booz & Company: http://www.strategyand.pwc.com/global/home/ what-we-think/reports-white-papers/article-display/ campaigns-capabilities-social-media-marketing

Russ, T. L. (2008). Communicating Change: A review and Critical Analysis of Programmatic and participatory implementation approaches. *Journal of change management*, 199-211.

Scott-Ladd, B., & Chan, C. C. (2004). Emotional intelligence and participation in decision-making. *Strategic Change*, 95-105.

Senge, P. (1990). *The Fifth Discipline: The Art and Practice of The Learning Organization*. London: Doubleday.

Shirky, C. (2011). *Here Comes Everybody: How Change Happens When People Come Together*. London: Penguin Books.

Smith, K. (2009). *A step-by-step guide to a successful social media program.* Marketingprofs.

Thompson, M., & Kahnweiler, W. (2002). An Exploratory Investigation of Learning Culture Theory and Employee Participation in Decision Making. *Human Resource Development Quarterly*, 271-88.

Wang, C., & Ahmed, P. (2003). Organisational learning: a critical review. *The learning organisation*, 8-17.

Watkins, K., & Marsick, V. (1993). Sculpting the learning organizational: consulting using action technologies. *New Direction for Adult and Continuing Education*, 81-90.

Wenger, E., McDermott, R., & Synder, W. (2002). *Cultivating communities of practice.* Boston: Harvard Business School Press.

ACKNOWLEDGEMENTS

It has been my pleasure to interact with some of the kindest and smartest people there are to know. Thanks to all those who supported me by providing me with their stories, advice and a listening ear throughout the creation of this book. Along with my family and friends, I'd like to thank the following people:

Mel Allan, Illustrator

Raphael Segun Awoseyin, Web Consultant, Époque Bleue

Rebecca "Becky" Edwards, Chief Communications Officer, GE Oil & Gas

Susan F. Emerick, Co-author, *The Most Powerful Brand on Earth*

Krista Kotrla, Senior Vice President Marketing, Block Imaging International

Enda Logan, CEO, The Fifth Business

Lucy McCarraher, Managing Editor, Rethink Press UK

Clare McNamara, Professional Coach, Move Ahead Global

David Rees, Executive Fellow, Henley Business School, University of Reading, UK

Kate Sullivan, Graphic Designer, The Fifth Business

Michael Smith, Director, Developed Edge

Alli Soule, Employee Engagement & Social Media Specialist, SAS

Todd Wilms, VP Digital, Communications & Brand at Verisign, Forbes Writer

INDEX

P

participatory change 15, 16, 81
Peter Senge 17
PostBeyond 13
Powering Collaboration' 93

R

realignment 3, 70, 77

S

Salesforce.com 43
SAP 11
SAS 52, 77, 123, 124, 125, 126, 127, 128, 129, 130, 131, 132, 133, 134, 135, 136, 137, 138, 139
shared vision. *See* Shared vision
Shared vision 18
Share of voice 94
social business hierarchy of needs. *See* social business readiness; *See* social business readiness
social business readiness 27
social capabilities 4
social characteristics 4
social media change 3, 20, 49, 73, 74, 78, 111, 116, 119, 121

social media managers xxii, 53, 116
social media mastery 27
social media programmes. *See* social programmes; *See* social programmes; *See* social programmes
social programmes 20, 21, 70, 82, 111, 140
Statoil 93
Sun Micro-systems 11
sustaining momentum 119

T

Team learning 18
Teams. *See* Team learning
technological foundations of Web 2.0 2
technological implementations 27
temporary change 25
Training 18, 19, 20, 105, 109
Twitter xxii, 12, 43, 44, 78, 83, 109

U

user-generated content 2

V

valuing 103

W

walk the talk 43

Y

YouTube 12

THE AUTHOR

Yekemi is Strategic Marketing Advisor at one of Lloyd's Register's businesses, LR Senergy. She leads the creation and implementation of strategic marketing initiatives for the  businesses' software products. As part of a developing brand and digital strategy, she is leading the early stages of an employee advocacy programme. Before joining LR Senergy, she worked for Schlumberger UK in various engineering, business development and marketing roles. She first became interested in the factors that drive employee participation in social media during her role as Senior Web Analyst at Schlumberger. Most recently, she worked for GE Oil & Gas as Senior Marketing Manager in the company's flexible pipes business, Wellstream.

Following an MBA (Distinction) from Henley Business School in 2012, Yekemi is now a part time Doctor of Business Administration student at University of Strathclyde, Glasgow. In her research, she examines the conditions for innovative outcomes in big data projects. She has spoken at the Society of Petroleum Engineers' Simplified Series and regularly publishes articles on LinkedIn and on her personal blog, http://thetaskmistress.me, where she writes about personal development, marketing and life's observations.

Yekemi has Bachelor's and Master's degrees in Chemical and Petroleum Engineering. She lives in Aberdeenshire, Scotland with her husband and two children.

To see more about Yekemi's work on employee advocacy, go to www.socialmediaparticipation.com.

You can also connect with her on LinkedIn, Google+ and follow @SmartSceptic on Twitter for tips and new insights on employee advocacy.

Lightning Source UK Ltd.
Milton Keynes UK
UKOW06f1940090516

273884UK00013B/132/P